Murders Unsolved

by Anthony Hunt

*Quercus

****
QuercuS
John Roberts
67, Cliffe Way, Warwick
CV34 5JG   01926 776363
john@walkwaysquercus.co.uk
www.walkwaysquercus.co.uk
****

Murders Unsolved

by Anthony Hunt

© Anthony Hunt

ISBN 1 898136 22 X

First Published 2002

Contents

The Author	ii
Thank You	ii
From Bertillion to DNA	1
The Police	3
In The News	6
Juries and Things	7
Illustrations	8
The Mysterious Mr Reeks (Bilston 1914 - Express & Star)	9
Murder on the Llandudno Express (Madeley 1889 - Daily Sentinel)	18
The Man in the Ulster Coat (Solihull 1880 – B'ham Daily Gazette)	24
Suicidal Coincidences (The Potteries 1893 - Staffordshire Sentinel)	29
The Blood Stained Shirt (Bilston 1884— Express & Star)	35
Not Another Day in Birmingham (Birmingham 1883 - B'ham Daily Gazette)	45
Highway Robbery (Birmingham 1817 - Aris's B'ham Gazette)	49
A Victim of Charity (Hanford 1877 - Daily Sentinel)	52
A Cap for Little Willie (Deepfields 1892 - Express & Star)	59
Bearing False Witness (Birmingham 1834 - Aris's B'ham Gazette	66
Poached to Death (Codsall 1887 - Express & Star)	72
Innocent as the Angels (Bradley 1857 - The Chronicle)	81
Stabbing in Fleet Street (Birmingham 1879 - B'ham Daily Gazette)	92
Kicked to Death (Longton 1887 - Daily Sentinel)	100
Muffled by Law (Wednesbury 1869 - The Chronicle)	103
A Life for Two Farthings (Wolverhampton 1902 - Express & Star)	112

The Author

Anthony Hunt was born in Hednesford east of Cannock in 1943. His first school was St Joseph's Primary at Hednesford, followed by St Chad's Grammar School, Wolverhampton. Heading for a teaching career, Tony spent three years at Dudley Teacher's Training College. After qualifying in 1964 he taught English and History in Staffordshire. He won a BA degree at the Open University in 1986 and took early retirement in 1994.

Tony's interests include writing, gardening and photography and he visits the elderly for his local church. Since he was a boy he has spent a lot of time on Cannock Chase, so the list of his interests includes natural history and walking. Having lived and worked all his life in South Staffordshire and next to the Chase, Tony has a special interest in the rich history of his area. He has written several articles on local topics for magazines, particularly *Best of British*. His trawls through archive material led him to local newspapers and murder, and to his first QuercuS title, *Accident, Manslaughter or Murder?*

Thank you

- once again to the calm and consiencious folk who help helpless researchers at the archive libraries of Hanley, Wolverhampton and Birmingham. They found everything I needed and put up with me so bravely.

Another thank you to Rob Cooper who chauffeured me about to all sorts of strange places on research and photographic expeditions.

Andy Tew remains just as mysterious and unknown to me as he was for my first book, but I do very much like his splendid illustrations to both books.

From Bertillon to DNA

When I started work seven years ago on a book of unsolved 19th century murders I thought it might be finished in a couple of years. But unsolved murders were extremely difficult to find. It seems there were remarkably few unsolved cases in the Victorian era because the police had an irritating knack of solving them. Even without the help of modern forensic science the Victorian police were successful in more than 90% of their cases.

What became clear as I read newspaper reports of old cases was that the police in any century have had one overriding advantage in dealing with murders - the vast majority are committed by people connected with the victim. Most common is murder by a spouse or partner when the man kills the woman while others are committed by the victim's relatives or friends.

Where the police have most difficulty is when the crime has obviously been committed by "person unknown to the victim", perhaps a random, opportunist killing where the motive might be sex or money. These are quite rare but even today they make up the majority of unsolved murders.

What makes the detection rate of the Victorian police so good is that they had to solve their murder cases without modern technology. Until the discovery in the 1880s that everyone has different fingerprints they used the Bertillon System, which identified people by their body measurements. But the fingerprint system was not fully developed until the 1890s and it was not until about 1910 (after most of the cases in this book) that it was widely used and replaced Bertillon.

In the Victorian age the police knew little about contamination of a murder scene. Today the forensic team "freeze" the area to take photographs and produce crime sketches recording the exact positions of each piece of evidence. They vacuum trap dust to collect trace evidence such as fibres, hairs, sand, wood splinters, glass and paint before anyone is allowed in. In Victorian times they didn't know the importance of such work and didn't have the techniques to deal with it, so some murderers got away.

Victorian police forces knew nothing about blood groups. While blood specimens cannot positively identify a criminal because millions of other people will belong to the same group, they might eliminate an innocent suspect. But it was not until the Austrian, Karl Landsteiner, discovered the four blood groups in the early 1900s that the police could use the knowledge in their work.

Today we have DNA fingerprinting or profiling. The hereditary information recorded in our DNA appears in all the cells of the body, making misidentification virtually impossible because no two people in the world are supposed to have the same DNA pattern. Some critics don't believe that this is yet totally certain or that the tests are completely accurate, and they question use of DNA evidence on its own.

The main source of police information in Victorian times, as now, was the general public. Cases never seemed to lack people willing to come forward even though they lived in violent places in violent times. Perhaps there was more respect for the police than there seems to be today, though the Willenhall Police might have argued with that during the 1860s when their officers were frequently attacked.

There were drawbacks in relying so heavily on the evidence of people closely involved. Prejudice against a suspect was always possible as you can see in the *Stabbing in Fleet Street* episode, and intimidation of witnesses was a definite danger. In the same case protection of criminals by friends was a problem. When the inhabitants of Fleet Street realised that the killer must be one of their own they refused the police any further help.

The Victorian police placed much greater reliance on rewards for information than police do today. Rewards in murder cases are not liked because they can produce witnesses interested only in the money, and the defence will not fail to take this up. In *Bearing False Witness* some witnesses invented evidence for cash, though they were never punished.

You might be led into believing that the police had one other difficulty, the law courts themselves, since many cases in this book show what seems to be obvious murderers getting away with it. However, the strength of our criminal justice system and the best protection for any one of us is that a person is innocent until they are proved guilty beyond doubt.

If the police of the time might be accused of any failing it would be the speed at which they brought prisoners to trial and often without enough evidence. Certainly in the last quarter of the 19th century the Wolverhampton Police were under great pressure as the number of unsolved cases grew and drew criticism from the press and leading citizens.

Whatever you think of the police forces of the day, their record in tracking down murderers was pretty good, probably 95%. Even today's forces with their modern techniques might be proud of that record, but they have improved on it and Staffordshire can boast of virtually 100% success.

The Police

Two cases in this book, *Bearing False Witness* and *Highway Robbery*, occurred before 1839 when modern police forces started yet constables of some sort were involved. What follows is a potted history of policing.

Justices of the Peace emerged after 1233 from commissioners appointed by the King to keep law and order in certain areas. Their main work was day to day policing and they appointed a high constable to supervise two constables per hundred, the unit of land used for administrative purposes. In 1344 a statute gave JPs permanent status and in 1368 they were given the powers of magistrates to try cases.

The unpaid constables came from the local communities and in theory all able bodied adult males were supposed to take turns at the work. In practice a great many men paid others to do their share. Shakespeare and some historians have painted the average constable as corrupt, ignorant and incompetent. Research shows that most of them were actually quite well educated and honest and competent enough to do the job

Most offences were very local, minor affairs that did not justify taking up time in the Assize Courts, so such cases would be heard by the justices, in ancient manor courts or local church courts. Many cases might well be dealt with informally by an employer threatening the sack, or by the priest.

From early mediaeval times until the mid 17th century criminal justice was largely local, amateur and often informal. When people usually lived and died in the same community and rarely travelled further than the nearest market town it seems to have met the needs of society.

London was always the biggest, busiest place and more likely to see crime and public disorder than anywhere else. At the same time it had fairly compact and effective local government with the resources to organise policing. As early as the 1200s the City was divided into twenty four wards, each having six watchmen under the supervision of an alderman. There was also the Marching Ward which patrolled generally and helped where needed.

These systems of policing probably more or less coped in the mediaeval period, but even before 1500 great changes had started. Overseas exploration, improved methods of shipbuilding and navigation, new approaches in agriculture, new industries – all made for a more restless, mobile society in a new mercantile age of trade and towns. In the 17th and

18th centuries enclosures of open land for the private use of big landowners and the new agriculture drove country people into the expanding towns where they scratched a living of sorts in the mines, factories and filth.

The old systems of policing were plainly inadequate, and the detection and suppression of crime came to be driven by draconian punishments for the felons and rewards for those who brought them to trial. The rewards were given by statute and encouraged bounty hunters and amateur associations "for the Prosecution of Felons".

The penalties were supposed to frighten off intended felons and by 1819 there were 223 capital offences. You might expect the list to include murder, treason and piracy, possibly rape and theft; they were all there alongside impersonating a Chelsea Pensioner and damaging Westminster Bridge. Hangings in the early 1800s were fewer than in the past, but they were very common and forty in a day was not unusual. None of this suppressed crime, of course, the felons were too desperate or too bold. Highwaymen, footpads, pickpockets, forgers, burglars, smugglers, poachers, horse thieves and sheep rustlers did a brisk trade. Rewards and penalties make no impression on people who don't think they will be caught.

The voluntary thief catchers, armed bands of the respectable, military style guards, watchmen and parish constables, did not prevent ordinary crimes, but still less could they cope with large scale public disorder.

Low wages, unemployment and high food prices lead to riots against factory machinery, enclosures, toll gates, rices and many other causes of grievance. The army was used but usually with surprising restraint. Suppression of riots rarely lead to excesses by the authorities and usually only a few ringleaders punished, often not severely. The courts often seemed to weigh the seriousness of the riot against the justice of the rioters' complaint and the disorder was almost tolerated as a necessary social safety valve.

Jonathan Wild was born in Wolverhampton in 1683, though I doubt that the city is proud of him. He was in turn buckle maker, ponce, brothel keeper and master fence under the guise of bounty hunting thief taker. At his Lost Property Office in London Wilde restored stolen goods to their rightful owners, for a "reward to be paid to the thief for handing them in", while his network of thieves brought a steady supply of new stock to the back door. Wild kept a register of thieves and their crimes, and when he had enough evidence to hang a man he put a red X against his name. After the execution he put another X, which is the likely origin of "double cross".

In 1748 Henry Fielding, lawyer and playwright (best known for *Tom Jones*), was appointed Magistrate for Westminster and Middlesex. Unusually for the time, he was not corrupt and managed to gather six other honest men around him who became known as the Bow Street Runners. Henry Fielding was succeeded by another honest and shrewd man, his blind brother, John, who held the same office for 25 years. In 1782 he formed a 68 strong Bow Street Foot Patrol which was the precursor to the Metropolitan Police.

In 1780 the anti-catholic Gordon Riots set central London alight, with the army shooting 250 rioters. This prompted a Bill which was set before Parliament in 1785 proposing an organised, paid police force for the City of London, Westminster and Southwark, but it was dropped. The City objected because it wanted to manage its own affairs (and still has its own police), but there was a general fear that such a force would be used by the government for oppression. Even so, the pressure mounted with the demobilisation of Wellington's army after the defeat of Napoleon in 1815 leading to massive unemployment and rioting. In 1819 a peaceable reform meeting at St Peter's Fields in Manchester lead to the yeomanry firing at the crowd and killing 11 people. The army was a very blunt instrument for controlling crowds; something less lethal, more permanent and more measured was needed.

In 1822 Robert Peel became Home Secretary and was able to promote his police bill which included much of the failed 1785 attempt. Entrenched opposition prevented him from taking it forward, but in 1829 he became Prime Minister with a sound majority and *The Metropolitan Police Improvement Act* became law. *The County Police Act 1839* allowed magistrates outside London to appoint a chief constable to recruit, train and organise local force, and in 1856 it became compulsory.

In April 1839 **Birmingham** Council were asked to vote the funds for a police force by raising a special rate, but they could not agree. However, that summer large Chartist meetings resulted in several serious riots and Parliament passed *An Act for Improving the Police in Birmingham*. Things moved so quickly after the abortive request to the Council that on 30th September 1839 a recruiting advertisement appeared in *Aris's Birmingham Gazette* and by 1840 the force was 320 strong.

The Black Country, the Potteries and all the countryside between fell within **Staffordshire** and the county police started in 1842 with a meeting of the Quarter Sessions Court in Stafford. A chief constable was in post by the end of the year and recruits were trained in the yard of Stafford prison. The three police districts covered the West Midlands, the Potteries, and the remaining rural areas including Stafford, Burton on Trent, Leek, Uttoxeter and Cannock. Lichfield and Newcastle under Lyme had their own police forces.

In the News

In my last book, *Accident, Manslaughter or Murder* (QuercuS, September 2001), I told of how I had started to research murders from copies of 19th century local newspapers. Inquests into unnatural deaths and the trials of people accused of causing them were lavishly reported, so they were a rich mine of information, speculation and condemnation.

The introduction to that book gives a brief history of the newspapers which I drew from. Not all of them crop up this time, but for readers who have not seen *Accident etc* (buy now, cheap at half the price) here is a summary with a note about other papers which only appear in this book.

Wolverhampton folk were reading *The Chronicle* from 1789. A Saturday supplement came out in 1855 and from this grew the *Midland Counties Saturday Express*. The *Evening Star* started separately in 1880 but the two papers amalgamated in 1884 to form the *Evening Express & Star,* and that plainly and obviously became the *Express & Star*.

In **Lichfield** the *Mercury* was launched in 1815 with a major report of the Battle of Waterloo. However it closed in 1833 and the modern paper grew from a revived *Mercury* started in 1877 by a Lichfield printer.

In the **Potteries** a paper with the neat title of the *Staffordshire Sentinel and Commercial and General Advertiser* was launched by a local printer in 1854 as a weekly. In 1876 an offshoot called the *Daily Sentinel* came out and it is now simply called *The Sentinel*.

Stafford had another venerable newspaper, the *Staffordshire Advertiser* launched in 1795. In a sense it continues in the shape of the *Stafford Chronicle* which took over the *Advertiser* in 1972.

Birmingham's most famous old paper and the most valuable for historians of the 19th century was *Aris's Birmingham Gazette* which started in 1741. The name changed in 1863 to the *Birmingham Daily Gazette* and it ran until 1956 when it sunk under competition from the *Birmingham Post* and the *Evening Mail*. Five stories in this book are based on reports in the two older papers, and I noticed that the author of another QuercuS book relied heavily on them. In *Coaching Days in the Midlands* Brian Haughton found news of new coach services, timetables, highway robbery, weather and accident reports.

Juries and Things

Since this is a book of unsolved murders most of the court proceedings are coroner's inquests into the time, place and cause of death, and there are only a few criminal trials before judge and jury. Again, in *Accident, Manslaughter or Murder* I gave an outline of the functions of the different courts. I don't wish to repeat the whole thing so here is a summary.

If the police wanted to hold a suspect, then as now, they had to take them before the local Magistrates' Courts. Victorian magistrates usually gave the police a week or longer before they had to return to ask for more time.

Once the police felt they had enough evidence they needed to bring the suspect to trial. All murders were tried before a judge and jury at the Assize Court in the County town, in these cases Stafford or Warwick; the modern equivalent is the Crown Court.

Before a person could be tried at the Assizes, as with the Crown Court today, they had to be committed for trial in the Magistrates' Court. Alternatively they might be indicted by the coroner's jury, see below.

The magistrates hearing these serious cases are not trying them to decide guilt or innocence but carrying out a sifting function. They hear the case for the prosecution and as much from the defence as that side wants to say at this stage, and from this they decide whether there is enough evidence to form a case for the accused to answer. The aim is to weed out hopeless and unjustified prosecutions and to tell the accused what he is charged with so that he can prepare a defence.

There used to be another route by which a person could be committed, which was by a coroner's jury. The coroner has existed since at least 1194 and over the centuries has performed various jobs, but by the 19th century they had only two. There was a minor duty to decide whether buried treasure was Treasure Trove and hence the property of the Crown, and their main work of investigating unnatural or violent deaths.

The coroner had, and still has, to establish the identity of the dead person and decide how, when and where they died. In Victorian times he had to summon a jury and could call whatever witnesses he thought might be helpful. The procedure is quite unlike any other court in the United Kingdom because it is inquisitorial. In other words, there are no sides, prosecution and defence, it is an investigation by the coroner. Both the coroner and the jury could question witnesses, and the jury often did so. People with an interest in a case such as relations of the dead person or someone accused of causing the death, could be represented and question witnesses at the coroner's discretion. The accused only had to appear before this court if they chose to and they could only be cross questioned with their agreement.

After the evidence had been heard the coroner would sum up the evidence and ask the jury to bring a verdict, which might be an open verdict or that the victim's death was caused by accident, suicide, murder or manslaughter. If they named the person they thought was responsible they issued a Bill of Indictment on which they could be sent for trial at the Assizes. Equally, the jury could decide that there was no case to answer.

Today the coroner hears most cases without a jury and although they may still say that death was caused unlawfully, they must not name anyone.

Illustrations

Apart from Andy Tew's sketches, which bring to life the people and the atmosphere of the times, we have used photographs of some surviving buildings and the invaluable Ordnance Survey maps.

These are worth looking at carefully, and you can take for granted that they were almost totally accurate. All the main roads and many minor ones, the railways and the canals appear as they do today. Most of the towns and villages are essentially the same although all have expanded. But look at the strange barren landscape in between these features, a wilderness of mine shafts, brickyards, foundries, pumping engines and tips that have completely vanished and which would not happen today.

We have also shown headlines from the newspapers. **Horrible Discovery near Madely** and **Extraordinary Occurrence at Soho Station** seem quaint and funny today the newsmens' urge towards screaming sensation strangled by grammar and verbosity. The state of the old copies was such that they could not easily be printed from, so what you see are reconstructions using typefaces as close to the originals as possible and exactly the same layout.

The Mysterious Mr Reeks
(Bilston 1914 - Express & Star)

This strange case has already appeared in *Midland Murders & Mysteries* by Barrie Roberts, the first QuercuS book of murder cases which was published in 1997. Since then prolonged and painstaking work amongst old newspaper files by Tony Hunt has revealed a little more of the background, but the result is to leave the mystery more baffling than ever.

At 8 o'clock on the bleak morning of 20th January 1914 little Elizabeth Hutton of 47 Mill Street, Bilston set off towards the Springvale Foundry carrying a wrapped pudding basin holding her father's cooked breakfast. Snowflakes blustered around her in the bitter wind as she crossed a piece of waste ground off Millfields Road. It was bounded on the west side by the Birmingham to Wolverhampton railway line and the Birmingham Canal, and on the east by the Dudley – Wolverhampton line. Elizabeth passed the brick wall around the mouth of a disused pit shaft where she saw a man lying in a shallow ditch. Thinking he was drunk or asleep she walked by, but told another girl, Mary Leadbetter. By 1 o'clock that afternoon the police had cordoned off the area and taken the body to the Bilston Mortuary.

The corpse was examined by Doctors Ashley Smith and G. Kendrick who found two bullet holes in the forehead and one in the right eye. Other than those the young man seemed to have been in perfect health and there were no other marks of violence. Under a blue plaid overcoat in naval style he had been wearing a bespoke serge suit with high quality underclothes, shirt and tie.

A letter found in an inside pocket was addressed to Mr. Kent Reeks, General Delivery, Boston, Mass., U.S.A. The contents were purely personal, writing of nothing more than family illnesses and Christmas. However, it was signed "Your loving Grannie Kent" who lived at 58 Chorley Road, Swinton, near Manchester and was dated 24th December 1913. The letter threw up another lead. Boston, Mass., USA. had been crossed out and the envelope re-addressed to the Liverpool Sorting Office from where it had been collected at 9.30am on 19th January 1914. The young man had left America before it arrived there and if he knew that the letter was in Liverpool then he must have visited his Granny some time before 19th January.

At Swinton on 21st January the police found four people living at 58 Chorley Road, Grannie Sarah Kent, an uncle - Thomas Kent, Richard Kent and his

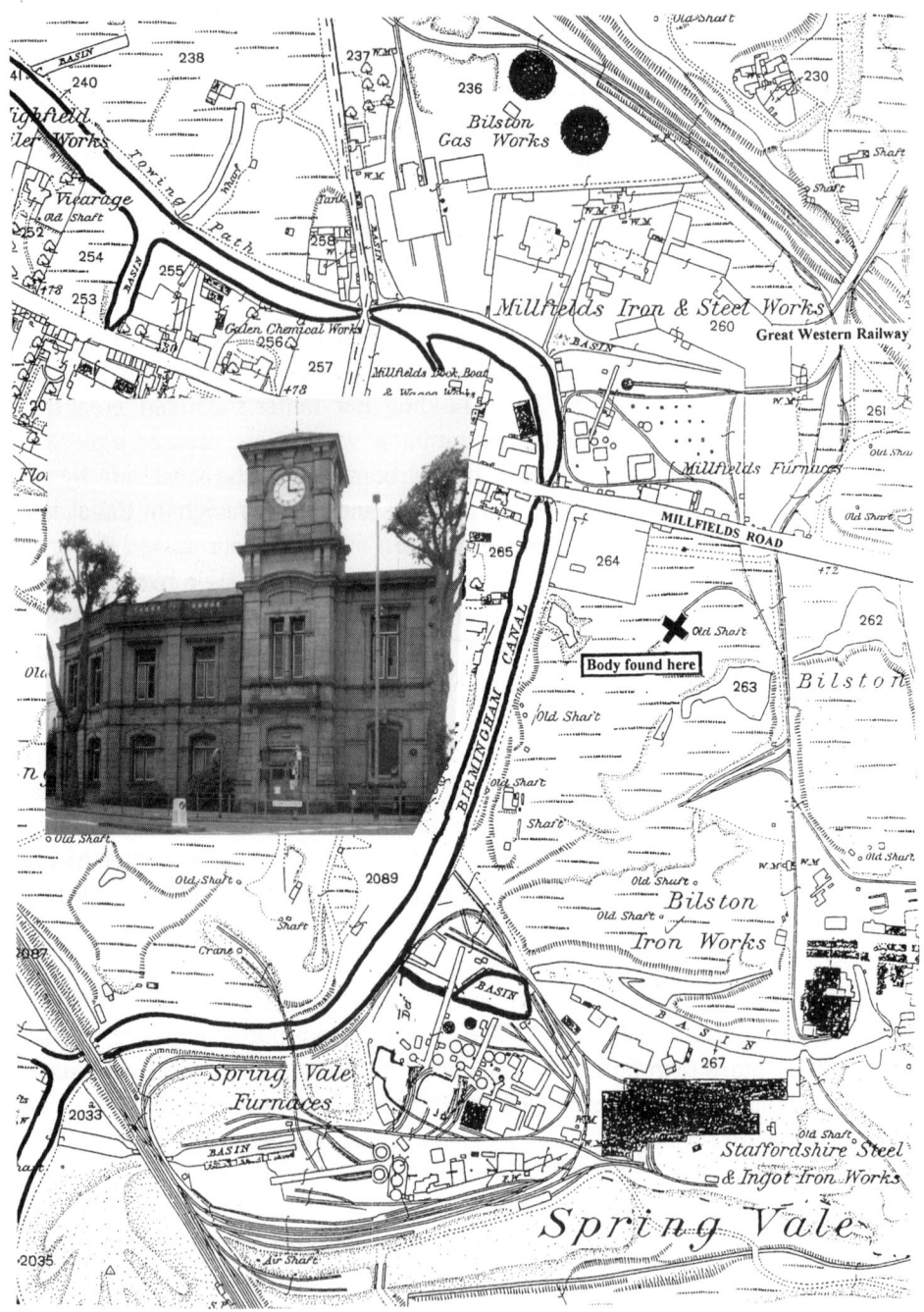

The 1887 Ordnance Survey map reduced from 6 inches to the mile shows a bleak wasteland of pit workings, brickfields and foundries broken by shafts, pumping engines, canals and railways. Inset is the grand, classical presence of Bilston Town Hall where the inquest was held.

wife. Grannie Kent had the first piece of surprising news - her grandson w neither British nor American but Australian. His mother had emigrated in the late 1880s to marry a Mr. Reeks, a ship designer, and in 1890 they had a son whom they christened Thomas Kent Reeks.

Kent Reeks had first visited England in 1911 when he was serving on the *Georgia* as an engineer. That ship was owned by the United Fruit Company of New Orleans, hence the American connection, and in the next two years he served on a number of the company's vessels. By late 1913 he had written to tell his relatives that he intended to come to England for a time to sit exams. for a British Engineer's Certificate, which would allow him greater career opportunities.

Uncle Thomas added that his nephew had sent a postcard from Boston telling them that he was about to leave for England, sailing from Halifax, Nova Scotia on the *Empress of Ireland*, and he would visit them as soon as he docked in Liverpool. He had landed on the morning of 17th January and after booking a room at the Temperance Hotel, Lord Nelson Street in Liverpool at around 11.30 am he left for Manchester. He had spent the afternoon with his family and returned to Liverpool in the early evening.

Uncle Thomas said that Kent Reeks had been in good spirits. His sister in law added that he seemed bright and cheerful and excited by the examinations he was going to take and his future prospects. He was in such a jovial mood that he did not even mind having his leg pulled about girlfriends. She remembered saying that he must have broken many hearts as he was so good looking, to which he replied that he would only "get married when I'm ninety".

Asked if they could think of any possible reason why their nephew might be attacked they could think of nothing because he was such a pleasant young man. However, they did remember that he had showed them a hundred dollar bill and they told him to keep it safely hidden.

[Given the inflation generated by 85 years of wars and trade crises we will not even attempt to guess what that $100 bill might represent today, but it must a have been a lot of money.]

This information did give the police a possible motive for the murder. A search of Kent Reeks's clothing had produced a considerable amount of valuables. There had been 9 gold sovereigns [coins worth £1.05 each], 2 shilling pieces [5 new pence each], an American 3 cent piece and a half penny [about ¼ of a modern penny], a great deal of money in those days. He had also a gold watch on a silver chain, a silver matchbox and a fountain pen. Because of the amount discovered the police had at first ruled out robbery, but the missing hundred dollar bill provided every reason for murder.

This left the police with another problem. Who would leave the cash and valuables and take only the American money? Except in London and the main Atlantic ports, dollars would be difficult to get rid of without arousing suspicion, unless the murderer were American and had travelled with Reeks. At last the police had a lead, but first Uncle Thomas had to accompany them back to Bilston to identify the body and give evidence at the inquest.

On 23rd January the coroner, Mr Stokes, opened the first hearing at Bilston Town Hall, but inquiries were proving so difficult that the only witness was Thomas Kent. He identified the body and retold the events of the afternoon of 17th January, adding that the last time that he saw his nephew was when he took him to Swinton Station and put him on an 8.30 pm train for Manchester

The Coroner adjourned the inquest and gave the police a further three weeks to come up with more satisfactory evidence. They would need all the time they could get because the case had captured the imagination of both press and public who were inundating the police with theories. Everyone, it seemed, wanted to play amateur detective. Most of this help only delayed inquiries, but every thread had to be investigated.

Press and public knew that the murderer might be American as the police had gone to Liverpool to inquire after Reeks's hotel companion, so anyone with American connections came under suspicion. A man who called at Cook's Travel Agency in Wolverhampton on the day of the murder and booked a passage to St. John's, New Brunswick became an obvious target. The *S.S. Grampian* had sailed so the police telegraphed the captain. He replied back:

S.S. Grampian at sea, Thursday 25th, 9.30 p.m.
The emigrant aboard denies knowledge of Thomas Kent Reeks. Evidently a mistake.
Captain Hall.

Later it emerged that the American Immigration Authorities had questioned the man further but released him. They had been suspicious because he had used a false name to book the ticket. However, Joseph

Rowland, alias "George Rogers", could prove beyond doubt that he could not have been the murderer because he had a perfect alibi.

Then a story surfaced (possibly from the police themselves) that Reeks had travelled under an assumed name. Was he a spy? Once again they had to investigate, but the passenger list of the *Empress of Ireland* which brought him to England on 17th January showed that Kent Reeks had travelled under his own name.

A BAFFLING CRIME.
STRANGE STORY OF A MOTOR CAR.
A CALL AT A WOLVERHAMPTON HOTEL.
BULLETS PURCHASED AT LIVERPOOL.
FUNERAL OF THE VICTIM TODAY.

AN ASSUMED NAME.
NEW PHASE IN THE BILSTON MYSTERY
A CONVERSATION ON THE ATLANTIC.
VICTIM'S WOUNDS NOT SELF INFLICTED.
WAS THE BODY DRAGGED TO THE PIT SHAFT?

BLACK COUNTRY MYSTERY.
RESUMED ENQUIRY INTO A BAFFLING CRIME.
A LIVERPOOL TELEGRAPH CLUE:
TWO AMERICAN SEAMEN WHO WIRED TO WOLVERHAMPTON.
VERDICT OF "WILFUL MURDER."

Express & Star Jan/Feb 1914

Staff of the Temperance Hotel in Liverpool mentioned Reeks being seen about with two men and two women. They seemed to have disappeared and there was no evidence that they had travelled on the *Empress of Ireland*. On the 19th January Kent Reeks told staff that he was about to set off on a journey, but none of them could remember him saying where he was going.

The press began to ask how the murderer had escaped from the scene and whether anyone had seen him? Once again the police had to eliminate possible sightings. Certain that the murderer must have used a motor car in his getaway, a story circulated that an employee of Wolverhampton Corporation had been stopped in Stafford Street at 6 o'clock on the morning of the murder by a driver asking the location of a pub where he had to pick up clients.

At about the same time two men called at the Little Swan, Horseley-fields, Wolverhamton and ordered a hot whisky apiece. They were perfect strangers to the landlord, so he kept an eye on them, but they vanished leaving their drinks untouched. Both men seemed to be in their early 50s and were respectably dressed, though they looked as if they had been up all night.

The landlord told his story to the police as well as to an *Express & Star* reporter, but nothing came of their enquiries. Another publican said that she had been awoken on the same Tuesday morning by a man asking for lodgings. As it was still very dark she only pushed back the curtains and told him that she had no rooms vacant. She could give no description because it was too dark.

Then the newspapers asked why Kent Reeks was in the Wolverhampton area at all? Did he have any relatives nearby? For once the police were a little more fortunate, but not for long. They did manage to track down the mother of Uncle Thomas's sister in law (not Richard's wife) whom Reeks might conceivably have been trying to visit. However, the sister in law had not lived at the last address known to the family in Swindon, near Dudley, for over thirty years and her mother, a Mrs. Cartwright, was a bed ridden old lady who had never seen the deceased. She did say that the young man had two uncles in the Potteries, one in London and another in Coventry, but did not know if they had ever seen their nephew. Police inquiries proved that they had not.

Another "clue" came from the Liverpool *Daily News*. Local gunsmiths, Hooton & James, had sold cartridges to two men on the morning of Monday 19th January, the day before the murder. One of the men answered the description of the dead man's friend, whom the police could not find. The other may well have been Kent Reeks. The first man was about 5ft. 11 inches tall and of medium build. He was clean shaven, with a rather fresh complexion, dark hair and wearing a dark overcoat. He was about 30 years old. The man with him was shorter, not so old and clean shaven.

The pair had bought 50 soft nosed cartridges and 50 solid ones. The shopkeeper told the newspaper reporter that he thought it odd as those cartridges were very powerful, especially the soft nosed ones which would make a "ghastly wound". He remembered the men clearly because the shop rarely sold that type of cartridge.

The police did investigate the story because the cartridges were similar to those found at the murder scene, but again they came to the conclusion that the two men who had bought them in Liverpool had nothing to do with the death of Kent Reeks. In view of the days and times given in later evidence, one wonders.

Despite all the help from the public and local newspapers progress was still very limited when the inquest sat again on 10th February 1914.

The first witness was Constable Felmingham of Ettingshall who told the court that the body had been found by a disused pitshaft some 84 yards from Millfields Road. The shaft had been capped by brickwork about eight feet high and a two foot deep trench dug all round it. That was where the victim's body lay. The head was covered with a coat and the left hand partly inside a pocket.

Examining the area he found three live cartridges and four spent ones within a distance of 45 yards. The three had apparently misfired. There was no sign of a revolver.

When asked whether Kent Reeks might have been killed somewhere else and dragged to the spot, the constable said that he thought it most unlikely because there were no signs of dragging. "It was a frosty morning, sir, and there were no signs of a struggle." Also the chain alongside the road was still fixed and "it was quite intact when I took it down". As to the use of a motor car to take the corpse to the spot, the constable said that there were no car tracks on the wasteland area.

This evidence was supported by Superintendent Robotham who told the hearing that the police had searched the murder scene again on 23rd January.

Then they had discovered a tie pin which they first thought might belong to the killer, but the uncle had recognised it as the one his nephew had shown to the family on his visit. There was still no sign of the murder weapon.

At the mortuary the corpse had been examined by two doctors and it was Dr. Ashley Smith who gave evidence next. He told the court that there had been considerable discoloration, probably due to the corpse lying face down in the ditch. On the forehead there were clean puncture wounds on the right side and near the centre. The left eye was completely destroyed and there was a wound on the top part of it. The bullets had penetrated the brain and one had lodged itself just inside the skull.

"And these wounds would cause instant death?" asked the coroner. Then came the ghastly reply, "Not immediate death, sir, but certainly very soon."

To the intent crowd at the hearing it began to sound as if poor Reeks was deliberately taken to this derelict place and executed. The murderer or murderers must have planned what he/they were about to do, but who might they be? Perhaps investigations in Liverpool might add further clues.

Catherine Stanton, keeper of the Temperance Hotel, 15 Lord Nelson Street, Liverpool was the next witness. Kent Reeks, she said, had booked into her hotel at 10 o'clock in the morning on 17th January asking for a bed for three nights. He had not said why he had come to England, but did say that he was going to Manchester to see relatives. After ten minutes he had left to buy a bag and was away for an hour and a half. Then he went out to buy another bag.

While he was away a man named Ramsden booked a room and said he would stay three nights.

"Was that man American?" asked the coroner.
"He did not appear to be American," said Mrs. Stanton, " but many Americans do not speak with an accent."
"And did Reeks meet Mr. Ramsden?" questioned a juror.
"They did not meet that day as Reeks went to Manchester," replied the landlady, "but they met on the Sunday morning [18th] at breakfast. During that meal they talked about the docks and the deceased showed Ramsden his discharge book. They went out together at about 10.30 and returned about 3.00. They had something to eat and then went out together again. Later they returned only to go out again."

She went on to tell the hearing that the two men breakfasted together again on Monday 19th January at 8.30, then while Reeks was in his room getting a handkerchief Ramsden left the hotel and Reeks followed him out. Ramsden returned on his own between 12 o'clock and 1 and asked for his bill, saying that he was going away to Leeds, but might be back in two or three days time.

Just after Ramsden had left Reeks returned and enquired after him. When he was told that Ramsden had left he said that he would also be going but would be back in two or three days. However, he only packed one bag, leaving the other behind. "That was the last we saw of him, sir," said Mrs. Stanton. "He left without paying his bill."

Uncle Thomas Kent had travelled to Bilston once more to give evidence. He said that his nephew knew no one in the Wolverhampton area and very few people in England, save for an aunt in London and a cousin in Bournemouth.

"Did he tell of any acquaintances made while on board ship?" asked the coroner.
"He mentioned that he had spoken to two lady passengers," replied Thomas, "but they were mere acquaintances, not friends. They were coming to England for a holiday."

So far as Uncle Thomas Kent could see, his nephew was most interested in getting back to Australia so that he could start a new life after his examinations.

The only other evidence heard was that of staff at Ettingshall Railway Station. Curiously they remembered two gentlemen leaving the train together though they could not describe either save that one "might answer the description of the deceased".

All evidence finished, the coroner summed up. It was "a most mysterious case. Although every inquiry had been made nothing whatever had been discovered. Absolutely nothing was known of the man from the time he left Liverpool until he was found at Ettingshall. But they could be in no doubt that it was a case of murder - of cruel murder too. However, I do not think any good will come of adjourning the inquest, unless the jury thinks otherwise."

The Jury did not and a verdict of wilful murder against some person or persons unknown was recorded. The police were left to try to gather more evidence, especially as to the whereabouts of Mr. Ramsden.

The vigilance of the press did throw up a few more tantalising clues. There was a telegram sent from Lime Street, Liverpool [terminus of the London & North Western Railway] to Wolverhampton on January 20th 1914 by a dark haired, tall clean shaven, young man with an air of the sea about him. But the leads all petered out and by that summer the Great War had started, pushing the fate of Thomas Kent Reeks into oblivion.

At Millfields Road the old mine shaft has vanished and the whole area has been developed for housing and clean, modern factories. The Birmingham to Wolverhampton railway line is electrified, the Dudley to Wolverhampton line is part disused, part tramway, and the canal is used only for pleasure boating.

Murder on the Llandudno Express?
(Madeley, nr Newcastle 1889 - Daily Sentinel)

The feature on steam trains which caused the greatest number of accidents was the carriage doors, which passengers opened themselves. The *Daily Sentinel* and other local papers ran many stories of people who had not realised how heavy those doors were or how quickly they flew open and had fallen from trains. However, when they ran the sedately titled story, *The Railway Accident in Madeley*, in August 1889 they were not at all certain about the cause. Did the victim fall or was she pushed?

Ann Davey, a 48 year old widow, left her home in Silverdale, Newcastle under Lyme on Sunday 5th August for a day excursion to Llandudno where she would visit a friend. It was quite an event in the life of a lady unused to travelling by train and alone. But the day passed pleasantly and when she was due to go home her friend escorted her back to Llandudno Station.

Mrs Davey never got home for on the morning of 6th August her mutilated corpse was found by the track near Madeley Road Station. This was on the Crewe-Stafford line about 3½ miles west of Silverdale.

Police moved her body to the Offley Arms where it was examined. Although the face and head were almost unrecognisable, the clothing helped with identification. She had dark hair and wore a light coloured stuff dress.

Underneath was a black and white petticoat and on the feet, elastic sided boots. On the fourth finger of the left hand were three brass rings and in one pocket was a small snuff box.

It was not long before the police knew the deceased's name because only hours before Mrs Davey's sons, William and Thomas, had reported their mother missing. After telling the police about their mother's trip to Llandudno they were taken to the Offley Arms and identified her body.

> **HORRIBLE DISCOVERY NEAR MADELEY.**
>
> ---
>
> **WOMAN FOUND ON THE RAILWAY.**

How would the paper's modern descendent, The Sentinel, write this headline?

It seemed quite straightforward - a tragic accident. But the sons discovered that some of their mother's belongings were missing. Where were her shawl, basket, umbrella and purse, containing quite a sum of money? None of these items had been found with the corpse. Suddenly the police were confronted with a possible robbery and murder. Had Mrs Davey been attacked and deliberately thrown from the train?

There was still the possibility that she had fallen and that her belongings might be found on the train or by the track, but inquiries raised some puzzling questions. The train which Ann Davey should have caught was bound for the Potteries via Crewe, but the London & North Western Railway Company inspected those carriages and found nothing.

Further inquiries revealed that there had been another excursion train to Llandudno that day which had run through the Potteries and finally stopped at Northampton. When the police contacted that station some of Ann Davey's items were found in the lost property room, but not all. The umbrella, purse and money were still missing.

Despite that, the police considered that Mrs Davey met her death accidentally. They presumed that she had boarded the wrong train at Llandudno but realised her mistake and tried to get off at Madeley Road, where the train did not stop. The missing items could simply have been taken by another passenger.

That theory did not answer some intriguing questions which surfaced at the inquest held on 22nd August 1889 at the Offley Arms. When Mr Booth, the coroner, opened the hearing he first remarked that investigations "had not resulted as satisfactory as they had wished". He apologised to the relatives for the time which had passed before the inquest could take place but he "still thought that the event of their mother's death was very mysterious".

First to give evidence was Jane Davey, Ann's daughter, who was unmarried and had lived with her mother at Chapel Street, Silverdale. She told the court that on the morning of Monday 5th August she had seen her mother before she left the house. She had not asked Jane to wait up that evening because she might be late home. When her mother left the house she had with her a bonnet, shawl and a basket of food for the journey.

Jane emphasised to the jury that her mother was not short of money. On the previous Saturday she had spent about 13 shillings [65p] on groceries and about 3 shillings [15p] at the butcher's. Altogether on that Saturday Mrs Davey had spent close on £1,6s.11d [£1.34] as well as 4s.6d [22.5p] on the railway ticket to Llandudno and still had money for the excursion, though Jane did not know exactly how much.

While certainly not well off, Mrs Davey was getting comfortably more than the average weekly wage of under £1.

Curiously, though not asked, Jane insisted on telling the jury that on the Saturday evening her mother had had a disagreement with her younger son, William, though she did not know the cause. It had led her mother to being "slightly in drink" later that evening. She had not drunk on the Sunday but gone to visit relations. Was Jane hinting that her younger brother might have something to do with the death?

If that were the case then police found no evidence. Sergeant John Marson said that they had checked the movements of both brothers, especially William, on the Sunday, Monday and Tuesday and they were thoroughly accounted for. Neither could be involved.

Sergeant Marson had been to Llandudno to check Mrs Davey's movements on 5th August. She arrived shortly before 1 o'clock and had been with Jane Owen until 5 pm. Both had gone to Llandudno Station where Mrs Davey said that she would catch the 6.30 train home. However, they arrived at the station an hour and a half early so Ann Davey said that she would visit Conwy where her parents had lived thirty years before as bridge keepers.

Mrs Owen told the sergeant that she did not know whether Mrs Davey knew anyone in Conwy, but presumed that she did as her friend was perfectly happy to go there. Mrs Davey had said that she was not worried about missing the train home because she had plenty of money to stay the night, though Mrs Owen saw none.

Sergeant Marson said that he had gone to Conwy but was unable to find anyone who knew or remembered Ann Davey. He had asked at cafes and public houses but could find no trace of her movements. Mrs Davey might simply have stayed on Llandudno Station and caught the 6.30 train, though there was no evidence of that.

The only other witness was Mr Peter Peters, District Inspector of the London & North Western Railway based at their Warrington office. He told the hearing that after inquiries some articles reported missing were found at Northampton Station. They had been left in a 3rd class carriage of a train which had been used for a Llandudno excursion on 5th August.

The train had been full as far as Stafford (south of Madeley Road) where a great many people got out to change for Birmingham. Mr Peters said he was sure that it would have been impossible to find an empty compartment on the train, hinting that any assault or jumping out was certain to have been witnessed.

That train had left Crewe at 12.27 pm and arrived at Stafford at 1.16 pm having stopped nowhere in between. There were no passenger trains on that slow line from Crewe to Stafford after that time and so it must be presumed that Mrs Davey could not have caught another train from Crewe that evening. In fact the next passenger train on the down line was at 11.40 am the next day, well after the body had been found.

As to how the body came to be on the line, Mr Peters was mystified. If a passenger door had been opened it would not have been shut again and the train would have been stopped and examined. No open doors had been reported. If someone had jumped there must have been witnesses; none had came forward. If someone had jumped how did the door close after them? If someone had been attacked passengers were sure to see it; no one had had reported any incident.

Mr Peters apologised to the court for the delay in examining the train for signs of blood. Inspections of all trains used that evening had produced nothing, but he had to admit that the weather and cleaning at the depot could have removed any such evidence.

With Mr Peters's evidence posing more mysteries, the coroner decided to conclude the inquest. He told the jury that nothing more could be gained from a further hearing and so advised them to return an "Open Verdict" adding that "it might be that Ann Davey had fallen asleep after taking off her bonnet and shawl. She could have been suddenly awakened and have thought of jumping off when she got to Madeley which is in the vicinity of Silverdale". He had to admit that it was all speculation and so the jury took his advice and recorded an "Open Verdict".

Nobody was satisfied with the outcome and the police continued to investigate the case. Eventually they drew the conclusion that Ann Davey's death was a tragic accident. But that left many unanswered questions.

One in my mind is why no medical evidence about the state of Ann Davey's body and the cause of her death was reported. Was she attacked? Did the coroner not think it necessary or was the evidence heard during the *Daily Sentinel* reporter's day off?

******

A strangely similar incident happened a year later at the Great Western Railway's Soho Station, Birmingham on 4th December 1890. It appeared in another QuercuS book, *Murder in the Midlands* published in 2000, but since then my delving about in old newspaper records has unearthed some new information from the *Birmingham Daily Gazette* and *The Weekly Mercury*.

As the 7.10 pm passenger train from Wolverhampton to Birmingham was passing through Soho Station the door of a third class carriage flew open and 21 year old Matilda Crawford fell onto the platform. The train was travelling at 40 mph and she was hurt, but according to my recently discovered newspaper accounts, her injuries were not serious.

EXTRAORDINARY OCCURRENCE AT SOHO STATION.

REMARKABLE ESCAPE FROM DEATH.

The story she told was chilling. She told Mr Rampton, stationmaster at Soho, that she had boarded the train at Wolverhampton with an aunt, a Mrs Chatfield of 13 York Street, Wolverhampton, who came to see her off. The carriage was not on the modern, open plan and did not even have a corridor. Each compartment was separate with its own door and once in, you stayed until the train stopped.

Before Matilda's train left Wolverhampton four young men entered her compartment and asked if they could smoke. When her aunt objected they were unhappy but found seats elsewhere. After her aunt left she was alone in the compartment, but at West Bromwich a man entered and began to make indecent proposals. When Matilda objected he pulled down the window, opened the door and threw her out.

Detective Inspector Monk and Sergeant Daniels began to investigate. Matilda's parents lived in Summer Lane, Ladywood, Birmingham and her father said that his daughter was prone to hallucinations and frequently imagined things happening. The mother added that Matilda suffered seizures which made her vague, though they lasted only for short periods.

The only witness who saw the girl on the train was Mr Collins, a railway detective who travelled in the next compartment. He said that he had noticed Matilda alone in her compartment and never saw anyone with her, and certainly no young man. However, he had not seen her "jump". Perhaps she had imagined the attack.

The police dropped their inquiries, but had Matilda Crawford imagined the attack or had she been assaulted? Either way she was lucky to escape with just a scratch on the hand and a bruise on the back of her head. Ann Davey, if attacked, was not so fortunate.

The Man in the Ulster Coat
(Solihull 1880 - Birmingham Daily Gazette)

If you were in a pub when one of the customers was killed, could you - would you, describe who did it? Perhaps the horror of the event might create a mental blockage, or perhaps there would be other reasons for forgetting. Something certainly affected the customers of the Gardener's Arms, Solihull in December 1880.

MYSTERIOUS OUTRAGE AT SOLIHULL.

ALLEDGED MURDER OF AN IRISHMAN.

The Irish connection was suggestive in view of Fenian activity at the time.

Twenty six year old Irishman, John Gateley from Colleen Olagh, Dysart, near Athlone, County Roscommon landed in England in 1874. Quite soon he found work as a cowman on a farm at Coleshill but in 1878 he moved to work for Mr Walter Graham, a well known horse breeder at Yardley, Birmingham.

As a devout Roman Catholic he went to Mass every Sunday at St Joseph's Church, Nechells Green, Birmingham. However, on Sunday 5th December 1880 he left Yardley at 9.00 am and walked to Stechford where he had arranged to meet another Irishman. He may have intended to go to Mass as usual but for some reason, possibly relating to the Irishman he had met, he entered the Gardener's Arms in High Street, Solihull at 1 o'clock. There he remained for three quarters of an hour, sitting with three strangers to the area. The remainder of the parlour was fairly full with customers, including many Irishmen who worked locally.

At around 2 o'clock Gateley left the parlour and went into the pub's back yard with two of the three men. Suddenly there was the sound of gunfire and John Gateley fell to the floor, clutching his stomach. In the panic that followed one of the men walked casually back through the parlour. The landlord asked him what was happening and he said that there had been an accident, then left the pub and disappeared.

The landlord went into the yard and found the bleeding Gateley lying on the ground. Immediately he called for the police and the local priest, Canon O'Sullivan. By the time that the police arrived almost half an hour had passed and all three of the strangers had disappeared.

Barely alive, Gateley was taken to the Workhouse Infirmary where an hour later, and knowing he was going to die, he spoke his last words. He did not name his attacker, in fact he said that he did not know the man and could give no positive description which might lead to an arrest. There had been no quarrel and the shot might just have been an accident. He died the following afternoon at 5.30.

The inquest opened at the Solihull Workhouse on 9th December 1880 under Mr Couchman, coroner for North Warwickshire. Police enquiries were no further forward and it seemed that the men who knew most about it had vanished from the area. The police had found particular difficulty in getting information from the drinkers in the Gardener's Arms. All said either that they had not noticed John Gateley and his three companions, or if they had they certainly did not know any of their names.

Michael Gateley was the dead man's brother. He told the hearing that he had come to England only recently and was working as a labourer in Widnes, Lancashire. He had last seen his brother in February on Mr Graham's farm at Stechford in Yardley. [The farm was in Yardley but Michael Gateley did not know Birmingham well so we can ignore his slightly confused geography.] He had learnt about John's death in a letter from one Michael McCale, whom he had never met, and had come to Solihull to identify the body. Unfortunately he could not tell the court the names of any of his brother's friends and was at a loss to know why anyone should want to kill him.

Dr ES Page told the court that he had been called to the Gardener's Arms on the Sunday afternoon where he found John Gateley lying on a bench. The victim had asked if he was a doctor and then said, "Doctor, I am shot. I am done for. I have nothing to do but prepare for Heaven." He was in great agony and complained of a pain in the abdomen and left hip. An examination of the wound revealed a hole to the right of the navel which seemed to be made by a bullet. Not having the necessary equipment with him Dr Page had the man taken to the Union Workhouse Infirmary.

When Gateley arrived there he was seen by Dr Palmer and Mr Rhodes. The passage of the bullet, they said, could be plainly traced through the dead man's clothes, and on probing the wound they found that the bullet had penetrated the abdominal cavity and lodged in the back muscles. Clearly he could not survive and they suggested that he make a deposition to the police. They could not be there immediately and so his dying statement was made in front of the two doctors, Canon O'Sullivan and Mr Madeley, Master of the Workhouse.

The deposition said very little which might help the inquest so the coroner decided that it need not be read out. He was more interested in the evidence from various witnesses.

James Bridge was landlord of the Gardener's Arms. He had been behind the bar when he heard what sounded like the report of a pistol. His barman, John Johnson, said that it sounded like a shutter banging to, but he disagreed. Before he could go into the back yard a man came from the yard and through the room. When asked what had happened outside he simply said, "I am afraid there is an accident."

"What did you do then?" asked the coroner.
"I went to the back yard, sir, and saw the deceased lying on his back in the yard. Realising that he was shot I asked the men in the bar to fetch a doctor and the police."
"And who were the men present?" asked the coroner.
"There were about a dozen Irishmen, sir, but I only knew one by name. He is called Ryan and works for Mr King at Hall Green. The rest work in the neighbourhood, two of them for Mr Chattock. There were also some Englishmen present, Fredrick Clark - a gardener, Joseph Green – a baker, and Richard Taylor."

Bridge said that he had not taken much notice of the man who passed through his bar and gave the message, and unfortunately could not give any description except that he might be about 5ft 4in tall and wore a long coat. "I was more interested in what had happened in the yard, sir."

The next witness was John Johnson, the barman. He said that at about 1 o'clock he had entered the parlour and seen John Gateley sitting with three strangers. The man who was supposed to have done the deed sat close to the door and wore a grey Ulster coat. He had overheard that man say to Gateley, "You must do something in this," but it had meant nothing to Johnson. Soon after the man in the Ulster coat and Gateley went into the street and had a long conversation, though the witness heard nothing of it.

When they came back into the pub Gateley went into the back yard where he was followed by the man in the Ulster coat and one of the others. Not long after Johnson heard a loud noise and thought it was a shutter, but following the landlord into the yard he saw John Gateley lying on his back.

Asked for a full description of the man in the Ulster coat, Johnson had more to say than his employer. "He had a pale face, with light sandy coloured whiskers. I thought he was about 30 years of age. He wore a grey Ulster coat with a short band and four buttons down the back and a hard billycock hat."

Johnson added that another man sat close to the four men and he was a Micheal Gateley (no relation of the brothers), an old man who worked for Mr Broadway. The only other thing Johnson remembered was that when the man in the Ulster coat left the pub he went in the direction of the station.

"Did no one take pains to follow the man?" asked the coroner.
"I don't know, sir," said Johnson. "I told my son to fetch the police and in about ten minutes they arrived and went after the man."

Johnson's estimate of ten minutes is at variance with the half hour mentioned earlier. This must have been how it seemed to the coroner who showed his displeasure with the police for their lack of speed in arriving at the scene. Constable Bastock gave an explanation. At the time there were only two officers on duty, the inspector being "upon the sick list". They were busy and went as soon as possible, but the three men had disappeared. An attempt to reach Superintendent Yardley at Acock's Green was foiled as the Acock's Green telegraph office was unoccupied.

Constable Bastock told the hearing that they had searched the roads leading to the station and were told that a man answering Ulster coat's description had passed the Barley Mow Inn heading towards the Birmingham Road. The barmaid there told the police that she had seen the man running past the corner of the inn and into Warwick Road. He was also seen at Olton on the route to Birmingham, but that was the last sighting in the area. A description had been circulated and they discovered that a man answering the description had spent the Sunday night in Birmingham at lodgings frequented by Irishmen. The following morning he had left by train for Liverpool, from where he seemed to have vanished.

The police had also interviewed the McCale brothers who turned out to be the other strangers sitting with Gateley in the Gardener's Arms. Both had known him well because they worked as cowmen on the same farm. They had been in the pub when Gateley entered, but both hotly denied knowing the man in the Ulster coat. According to Michael McCale that man knew John Gateley because he had visited the farm several times, but only to remonstrate with him. Michael McCale thought that the arguments had been about collecting money for the Irish Land League though he would not swear to it.

There had long been movements for Irish independence but during the 1860s new ones emerged. These included the Fenian Irish, the Home Rule Party and the Land League, whose main aim was to gain private ownership of land by the Irish peasantry. They have been described as a potent mixture of physical and moral force.

Michael McCale also admitted to being the brother who followed the deceased into the yard, but swore that he did not know what was about to happen. He had been shocked and frightened by the murder and had escaped in case his own life was in danger.

"Despite further questioning, sir," added Constable Bastock, both brothers maintained their ignorance of the man and are even today frightened to leave their lodgings."

"But they might be requested to give evidence at any subsequent hearing," said the coroner. In fact they were not called again because there seemed no reason to doubt their truthfulness.

The final witness at the hearing was Phoebe Atkin, domestic servant to the pub landlord, James Bridge. On hearing the pistol shot she ran into the yard to see the man in the Ulster coat holding a pistol and John Gateley standing by his side. It seemed as if he would fall and the Ulster coat man said, "What is the matter?" Gateley said, "I am done for." He appeared to go towards the other who turned and left the yard. Frightened, Phoebe went inside and told her mistress about the shooting.

After Phoebe's evidence the coroner advised the jury to find a verdict of "Murder committed by person unknown", which they did. He closed the inquest and hoped the police might have more success in their investigations.

So, what are we now to make of John Gateley's dying statement? Did he really not know the man in the Ulster coat, had there been no quarrel, and could it possibly have been an accident?

The police never did find the man in the Ulster coat. Despite continued attempts to persuade the customers of the Gardener's Arms to co-operate, all denied any knowledge of him and seemed too frightened to say anything. Rumour had it that John Gateley was killed because he had pocketed money collected for the Irish Land League and his death or execution was a warning to others, but that was never proved.

Suicidal Coincidences?
(The Potteries 1893 - Staffordshire Sentinel)

On 27th January 1893 the *Staffordshire Sentinel* ran a story headed in their usual restrained style, "The Mysterious Disappearance of Girls". The reporter could not have guessed what was about to happen. Of the four young women mentioned, two literally surfaced within days of each other in local stretches of water. Whilst suicide was suspected, similarities in their deaths suggested something more sinister.

Mary Sillitoe, a 16 year old from 13 Velvet Street, Burslem was last seen by her mother, Ann, on the morning of 16th January when she left the girl at home to go to work at Wilkinson's Central Potteries. Mary was finishing her breakfast before following her mother to the works, but she never arrived.

Although mother and daughter sometimes worked together, that particular week they were at opposite ends of the factory. It was only when Mary did not return home that Ann began to think that something might be wrong.

Thinking her daughter might have spent the evening at a friend's house, it was not until the next day that she reported the disappearance to the police.

By 19th January the police were concerned for Mary's safety, but enquiries produced nothing. It was only three weeks later that her corpse was found floating in the Burslem Branch of the Trent & Mersey Canal near Middleport. Suicide was the most obvious conclusion, but the inquest held at the Leopard Hotel, Burslem on 8th February uncovered disturbing facts.

Ann Sillitoe told the hearing that she knew of no reason why her daughter should commit suicide. Although they lived a simple life, the family was fairly comfortable because both women had regular work and earned enough to keep themselves and the other children. The father did not live at home, he had been "tramping" for 13 years, but he was always kind and did his best where possible.

When questioned by Mr Booth, the coroner, Mrs Sillitoe said that she and her daughter rarely quarrelled. There had been a slight disagreement on the evening of Sunday 15th January when Mary had forgotten to put the children to bed, but it was such a minor argument it would hardly have led to suicide.

"Do you think that your daughter committed suicide?" asked Mr Booth.
"I have not the slightest idea, sir," replied Ann. "All I know is that she was not in trouble [pregnant], nor had she quarrelled with anyone else or with her sweetheart. In fact she was a good girl, with the exception of her hasty temper."

The hasty temper was mentioned by various witnesses. Ann Elizabeth Kinney, Mary's best friend, lived at 70 Church Street, Burslem. She told the hearing that they worked at the same factory and had been good friends for nearly 4 years. They saw one another seven or eight times each week and confided in one another. Ann was certain that on no occasion had Mary complained of her mother.

"Mary was a very quiet and happy girl," said Ann, "though her one fault was the hasty temper. But never with me."

On the evening of Sunday 15th January they had been out together from 7.30. They had planned to go to the local chapel where Mary was a choir member, but Ann was late getting ready so instead they had walked into Burslem and back. By about 9.30 they arrived back in Velvet Street and at 10 o'clock Ann left to go home. All evening Mary appeared "just as usual".

When asked about the Burslem Branch of the canal Ann said that they had been there, but it had been about 3 years ago and they "were never in the habit of going there now". Why Mary should be there Ann could not imagine because it would be "an unusual way for her to go".

Questioned about Mary's sweetheart, Ann said that her friend had not seen him since just after the Christmas period. She had not mentioned him on that evening and had not received any letters since Christmas. She was sure that Mary was not in trouble with him or because of him.

The next witness was that boyfriend. Walter Arthur Wynn told the court that he had last seen Mary on 3rd January when he had stayed at her house. He had not been able to see her since because he was a sailor on the *Vernon*. During his stay she had seemed fine. The two of them had not quarrelled and he knew of no reason for suicide. Unlike the others he had never witnessed Mary's temper or any sulky behaviour; she always appeared happy.

The coroner's jury were puzzled. So far they had heard of a happy girl with no reason to kill herself. Was there more to the death than at first seemed possible?

Abraham Gibson, a miner living at 103 Slater Street, Middleport, had discovered the body close to Jones's Mill. At first he had only seen the hair, but when a boat passed the body drifted closer. He had called Constable Brawn to the scene and the two had taken it to the house of Lavinia Hollingshead, a widow of 9 Bell Street, Burslem who was a neighbour of the Sillitoe's house.

Unfortunately before it could be examined by a police surgeon, Lavinia Hollinshed had washed the body and arranged it so that it would look better when Mrs Sillitoe came to see it. Had she accidentally wiped away any traces of an attack?

Then there was the place where Mary's corpse was found. Witnesses said that the pathway nearby was very wide and an accidental fall into the water would have been impossible. That particular pathway was also "much frequented" and suicide would have to be carefully planned. Mary did not seem the type. Then again, an attack on a lone girl would be very risky.

The coroner admitted that he was puzzled by the death, as well he might be, but strangely, no medical evidence seems to have been heard. I say "seems" because it might be that it was heard but not reported by *The Sentinel*, though usually newspapers welcomed all such copy that they could get.

The coroner advised the jury to record a verdict of "Found Drowned", hoping that the police might come up with further evidence. However, they barely had time to begin investigations before a second corpse was taken from the water.

On 31st January 1893 15 year old Hannah Bough left home at 13 Newhall Road, Normacot, Longton on an errand for her father. She was taking 3 shillings rent money [15p] to their landlord, Mr Thomas Mollart. She arrived at his house in Weston Road, The Meir shortly after 6.30 pm, paid the rent and had it signed for, then pocketed the rent book and left. She was not seen again until her corpse was dragged from the pool at Cinderhill at about midday on 23rd February.

The inquest which opened on Thursday 25th February at the Newtown Hotel, Longton began to reveal alarming coincidences between Hannah's death and that of Mary Sillitoe. Once again the court was to hear of a young girl with no obvious motive for suicide. Like Mary, Hannah was in no trouble and had not quarrelled with her family. Like Mary, she appeared to be perfectly happy.

James Bough, Hannah's father, said that he gave his daughter the rent money as usual and she left the house at about 6.30 pm. When she had not arrived back he went to The Meir to look for her. Having found that she had paid the rent and left he searched the local streets, but when she had not come home by late evening he reported her missing to Superintendent Evans. He did not see Hannah again until he was called to Catherine Smith's home to identify the body.

Hannah "always appeared to be in good spirits" and even though he had six other children she never quarrelled with any of them. The only other thing that he could tell the court was that Hannah's hat and shawl were missing when he saw the corpse.

Mr Mollart confirmed that Hannah had indeed arrived at his home at around 6.30 on 31st January and paid the rent. He had watched her walk down the yard as she left and remembered that she turned in the direction of Weston Coyney Road. He knew nothing more until James Bough came looking for Hannah and he helped in the search.

Hannah's movements after she left The Meir would never be known, but what happened to her body after it left the water and before the doctor had time to examine it was a forensic nightmare. There was also a weird parallel with what had happened to the corpse of Mary Sillitoe.

At miday on 23rd February Catherine Smith's young son was playing near the edge of Cinderhill Pool when he thought he saw a dead dog in the water. He called his mother from nearby Cinderhill Cottage and she noticed floating hair. Seeing that it was no dog, she collected her clothes prop and managed to hook the body and pull it to the bank. With her husband she dragged it clear of the water, placed it on an old door frame and carried it to their yard.

Knowing that James Bough's daughter was missing they sent for him. After his identification the body was taken to Mary Titterton's home so that she could "arrange" it. It was only after she had done so that the police surgeon was called and started to examine the body at 9.30 that evening, some nine hours after it had been found.

Members of the jury questioned Catherine, as such jury's could do, about the condition of the body. She said she noticed that the lower clothes were all torn from their waistbands, but the underclothes seemed untouched. The upper garments, including a blue striped jacket, had not been touched.

Mary Titterton said that there was a lot of dirt on the corpse from the sludge in the pool. She had washed it off and noticed a small red mark on the lower part of the body. She, too, was certain that Hannah had not been sexually molested as "there was no appearance of violation about the lower part of the deceased's body". Her underclothes were in their "natural position".

Dr Arthur Price, the police surgeon, said that the body was laid out when he arrived at Mrs Titterton's. On examination he could find no marks of violence or sign of anything improper having occurred. Because the corpse had mud in the hands (Mrs Titterton had told him) and froth about the mouth (per Mrs Smith) he thought that Hannah had gone into the water alive and had drowned. The red mark mentioned by Mary Titterton was, he thought, "simply discoloration which would be caused after death". Strangely he was not asked how that might occur. Even stranger was the fact that he made no mention of rope marks found on Hannah's arm, a fact which only came to light when Superintendent Evans gave evidence.

Evans told the hearing that all investigations concerning the rope had drawn a blank and so the police presumed Hannah had tied it to herself. As to the missing hat and shawl, it was suggested by one officer, Sergeant Leese, that the girl had gone into the wintry water which had later frozen over. When it thawed the water had risen and washed the garments downstream. However, the police had dragged the pool and brook but found nothing.

To clarify the rope puzzle the coroner recalled Mrs Smith who explained that when she took the corpse from the water there was some cord wrapped around the girl's arm. It was about a foot long and tied to a tree bough. It appeared to be the type used for pulling a barrow. [I have no idea what that would be like.] Mrs Smith had removed it and given it to the police.

There were no further witnesses so the coroner summed up. It "appeared to be a very mysterious case". How the girl came to be in the pool "was impossible for anyone to tell", but he thought violence was unlikely. "As far as the rope was concerned it seemed a very peculiar circumstance", but perhaps the girl tied herself to the bough to weigh herself down. Since wood floats this was a very odd comment. Finally he said that as there was no definite evidence as to how the body got into the water he had no option but to advise the jury to find a verdict of "Found Drowned", which they did.

So a second case within weeks had proved baffling. Had both girls committed suicide or was something more sinister happening? As *The Sentinel* reported, Mary Sillitoe and Hannah Bough were not the only ones to die mysteriously in the Midlands in the January of 1893. Mary Henrietta Sherwin of 4 Oxford Villas, New Oscott, Perry Barr and Annie Braithwaite of Stockport both went missing and were later discovered drowned.

The Blood Stained Shirt
(Bilston 1884 - Express & Star)

Between 8 and 9 o'clock on the morning of 3rd January 1884 the body of a young woman was found lying on a cinder heap. Eliza Cartwright, a 21 year old brickmaker who lived with her parents in Chell Street, Bradley had suffered a terrible attack in this desolate place at Deepfields, between Wolverhampton and Bilston. Despite her injuries the girl was still alive and she was carried to the nearby Anchor Inn where the police surgeon, Mr Clendinnen, made a quick examination. Realising her desperate condition he quickly had her moved to Wolverhampton General Hospital, but despite the efforts of staff she never regained consciousness and soon died.

> **MURDEROUS ASSAULT AT DEEPFIELDS.**

Close examination showed that Eliza had been battered severely about the head and body, possibly in an attempted rape. The police had to act quickly and find the attacker before he could strike again, and at first the news brought a speedy response and many witnesses.

On the afternoon of 3rd January a little girl was walking along the road from Bilston to Wolverhampton when youthful curiosity took her into a derelict cottage near the bridge over the Great Western Railway. On the floor of the cottage she discovered a man's shirt which had obviously just been dumped because it was still warm. Thinking it very strange, the girl took the shirt to the local police station where it was examined by Constable Navington.

There were blood stains on the sleeve and lower part of the front. Having already been notified of the murder at Deepfields, the constable sent the shirt to Chief Superintendent Longden at Bilston Station. There it was noted that the shirt had been made in Oxford and had a pattern of diagonal green stripes. It should be easy to trace the shop where it was bought.

The shirt could be the vital lead the police were looking for, but could they find its owner? On the evening of Friday 4th January a Mr Meese of 7, Waterloo Street, Bilston Road, Wolverhampton, contacted them after reading about the murder in the *Evening Express*. He told the police at Monmore Green Station about a tramp who had called at his home that day asking for help. The man was about 5 feet 9 inches tall, dressed in grey tweed and had slight whiskers. What made Mr Meese suspicious was the man's strange request. The beggar had particularly asked for a shirt, saying that his own had gone missing two days before.

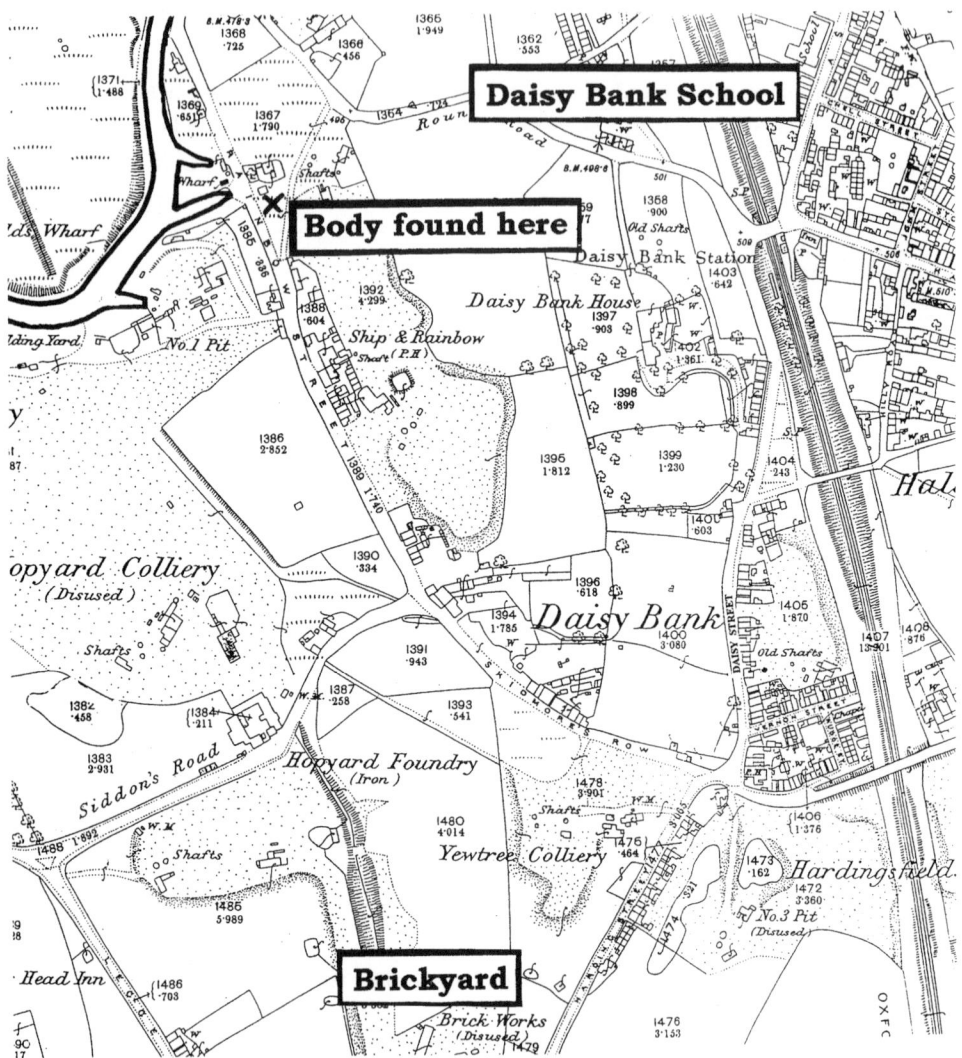

From the 1887 Ordnance Survey map. Note Chell Street just right of the school.

Was that vagrant their killer? They seemed to have a definite lead, but despite all their efforts they were never to find him. They visited the local works to ask if anyone knew of passing labourers looking for odd jobs, they searched all the known pit hovels and disused engine houses and they visited all the known poorhouses in case he had looked for lodgings. In short they scoured the entire area, but found nothing. Even the lead on the shirt ran dry because the shopowners did not keep records of people who bought small items like shirts.

Nearby police forces were told about the tramp and asked to keep a look out, and it was from the Worcester Police that they had a possible lead. In the previous year one Thomas Moore had been questioned for a similar assault on a female, though she had not been beaten up. He had absconded from Worcester and was thought to have headed for Wolverhampton.

Moore was described as around 32 years old, 5 feet 9 inches tall, with dark hair, thin face and sallow complexion. He was of rather slender build and considered "rough looking". He usually worked as a labourer, but sometimes sold herbs in local markets. In the evenings he usually frequented "low beerhouses".

But if Moore was their murderer, and there was never clear evidence that he was, then he was not to be found in Wolverhampton. Numerous searches and interviews of local "criminals" never turned up the slightest hint of his having been there.

When the inquest took place on 5th January 1884 at the New Market Hotel, Cleveland Road, Wolverhampton under the coroner, Mr W.H. Phillips, the police were no further forward. Could any of the witnesses summoned to the hearing throw light on the case? The police had not dismissed the possibility that someone who knew Eliza might be responsible, but successive witnesses seemed to rule that out.

Mary Gladders of 9 Chell Street gave a glowing report of the Cartwright family, especially Eliza. She had known the girl for many years and to the best of her knowledge Eliza had never had any male acquaintances, nor expressed any wish to have any. Eliza was happy to live with her mother and stepfather, John Ball, and they did so "very agreeably". Eliza had worked at Mr B Whitehouse's Brickyard as a clay carrier and seemed to be happy there. To Mary's knowledge she had not complained about her work.

On the evening of 2nd January Eliza had been with Mrs Gladders cleaning Daisy Bank Board School. She had arrived there after her own work to help with the cleaning and had relieved her mother who had been there all day. Mrs Ball had gone home to prepare a meal. Eliza seemed perfectly happy and at 10.45 they both left the school and walked together to Chell Street.

On arriving home Mary Gladders remembered that she had promised Eliza a pair of boots for work, so she took them next door and gave them to Mrs Ball. Eliza was at home as usual and Mary Gladders heard her in the next room, though she did not see her. The following morning between 8 and 9 o'clock she was told of the dreadful attack on the girl, and because she was such a close family friend she went with Mrs Ball to the hospital.

When she saw Eliza she was still alive, but unconscious. The girl was wearing the same dress as the day before but it was spattered with blood. Also Mary noticed that Eliza was wearing the boots which she had given to Mrs Ball the night before.

Mary Gladders could offer no reason to why the girl had been so savagely attacked. Neither could the next witness, Sarah Ball. She told the hearing that she and Eliza's father, Samuel Cartwright, had separated some eighteen years ago and she had gone with her daughter to live with John Ball. During that time Samuel, a waggoner at Bilston, had died and so she had married John Ball. Eliza had lived happily with them and there had never been any arguments about these arrangements.

Neither was her daughter unhappy with her job in the brickyard. She had worked in several brickyards over the last three years, and for the past six months had been at Mr Whitehouse's yard in Deepfields. Eliza usually left for work at around 6.30 am and always walked there alone so far as Mrs Ball knew. In the evening she walked home alone because there was no one nearby who worked at the same place.

Eliza had never worried about going to work alone, even in the dark, though she had told her mother of an incident some six months past. Eliza had been alarmed by a strange man "running almost on his hands and knees across a field". He seemed to be heading straight for her and so she had run up to two men who were close by. That had happened by the Black Horse Inn near Darkhouse Lane. Eliza had changed her route to work and seemed to have forgotten about it because she never mentioned the incident again.

On the evening of 2nd January Eliza had stayed up until about 1.30 when John Ball returned from work. He was a miner at the Daisy Bank Colliery. The following morning he had called Eliza just before 7 o'clock. She had overslept and left the house just as the "bull" was blowing at Mr Perry's Works nearby. The "bull" was the hooter or whistle telling workers that the factory was about to start. Mr Perry's whistle always went off at 7 o'clock.

"Even though she were late, sir", continued Mrs Ball tearfully, "Eliza still had time to shout 'Good morning, mother,' as she left."

"And what of Mr Ball?" asked the coroner.

"Oh, he returned to bed. He was on nights at the pit that week," explained Mrs Ball.

Not wishing to cause Mrs Ball any more distress, the coroner let her stand down. The next witness's evidence was the most disquieting and caused the most local outrage.

Mr Batterham, the hospital house surgeon, told the court that he had examined Eliza Cartwright when she arrived in hospital. She had multiple injuries to her hands and face as well as the back of her head caused by a large rough object. A cinder lump would be a likely weapon.

As Eliza was "muscular and well-nourished" she must have put up quite a struggle which would account for the number of wounds as the murderer tried to force her to submit. Mr Batterham could only suggest that the attacker had tried to rape the girl, and when she fought him off he went on to batter her to death. The attack would have taken several minutes and moved over a considerable distance as Eliza tried to escape.

Those facts were confirmed when several witnesses described the murder scene. Thomas Lewis, a postman, had walked by the canal to Rainbow Street and had arrived at the Blue Button Engine [water pumping engine for the Blue Button Colliery] at about 7.45.

The first thing he saw was Eliza Cartwright's clothing scattered around the cinder bank. Then he came upon the girl in a hole at the bottom of a slope. As he arrived he thought he heard her groan, but when he spoke to her there was no reply. When he saw the pool of blood he feared the worst and ran for help to Holcroft's Cement Works. So sickened by the sight was Lewis that he refused to return to the scene and left some Holcroft workers to see if the girl was dead.

Joseph Rollasop, a bricklayer at the works, and his brother went to the scene. He told the hearing that 30 yards from the scene he noticed blood stains and footprints on the ground. He followed the stains and found a handkerchief in which the deceased had wrapped her breakfast. Then they came upon the murder victim lying in a pool of blood. It was Joseph himself who found the cinder lump, almost a foot long, covered in a great deal of blood. They had not been there long when Constable George Jackson arrived.

Quickly examining the body, the constable realised that the girl was still alive, but only just. She was carefully taken to the Anchor Inn while he stayed behind to examine the area. Eliza's battle to save herself had ranged over some 37 yards. The place were she was battered in the final struggle was 14 yards from where her attacker had dumped her body down an embankment. In searching the surrounding area PC Jackson found a shawl which had been torn in two, and an apron. Young Eliza had put up a courageous fight.

With this evidence recorded the coroner adjourned the inquest saying that the police should do everything in their power to arrest the murderer.

When the coroner resumed on 18th January the police had made no progress and the only new witness was Emma Cartwright, Eliza's half sister. She was born not long after Mrs Ball moved in with John Ball and she still lived at home. She shared a bedroom with Eliza and on the evening of 2nd January had also waited up for John. They had both risen the following morning after Mr Ball had called them, but she had remained at home that day.

She repeated the incident of the man who had frightened Eliza and explained how, tragically, Eliza had changed her route to work to pass Green Gate Lane and the Blue Button Colliery.

Emma had been at home when Henry Rogers arrived and told them that Eliza had been "almost murdered".

"And where was your step father?" the coroner asked suddenly as if to throw Emma off guard.

"In bed, sir," came the instant reply. "He had gone back to bed after he woke up Eliza and me. He was still there when Henry Rogers arrived."

Finally Emma said that to her knowledge her sister had not quarrelled with anyone. She had never kept company with men, nor had she ever spoken of being molested by anyone. At work she never rowed with anyone and was well liked by them all. In fact Emma found it difficult to believe that anyone would want to harm such "a quiet and pleasant girl".

The coroner had established when, where and how Eliza Cartwright had died. After conferring with Chief Inspector Logan who was in charge of the case there seemed no immediate prospect of identifying any suspect and therefore no point in continuing the inquest. He instructed the jury to return a verdict of "wilful murder by a person or persons unknown", and the jury complied, adding that they thought the government should offer a substantial reward for the discovery of the guilty party or parties.

Four days later the police arrested two tramps at Hanley, Stoke on Trent and charged them with vagrancy. William Fereday and Enoch Price, alias Horton, were suspected for several reasons of being concerned with Eliza's death.

When arrested while sleeping rough in a brickyard at Trent Vale, Price gave a false name and he had blood stains on his clothing. Both he and Fereday admitted to being in the Bilston area at about the time of the murder and to having lodged near to where the crime was committed. They were immediately sent to Bilston Police Station and questioned, but after lengthy and thorough interviews they were released.

Eliza's murderer seemed to have escaped and the police scaled down their investigations, though never giving up hope. Then twelve years later on 26th July 1896 a new lead appeared.

At about 11.40 on that Sunday evening 30 year old Isaac Doughty met Constable Beardsmore in Hampstead Street, Handsworth, Birmingham and said that he wanted to give himself up for a murder in Bilston many years before. He was immediately taken to Thornhill Road Police Station where he was interviewed by Sergeant Hayward, who had been involved in the original investigation into Eliza Cartwright's death.

Doughty said that he wanted to get the crime off his mind and willingly made this confession:

> "I, the undersigned, Isaac Doughty, of Chell Street, Bradley, near Bilston, surrender and make a confession that on November 26th, 1885 as near as I can remember in the company of a man named William Davies, an underhand puddler, who lived at Daisy Bank, and who died about six years ago and was buried in Coseley Churchyard, met Eliza Cartwright, who lived with her parents in Chell Street, Bradley, as she was going to work at Whitehouse's Brickyard, Deepfields at about six o'clock or six-thirty.
>
> I took hold of her near the Blue Button Canal Bridge. It was breaking daylight. I said to her, "Who bist [are] thee going to have out of we two?" Davies had at that time come up to us. She replied, "Neither of you." and so I struck on the head with a cinder and then Davies struck her on the head with another cinder. We thumped and thumped her until she fell. We then heard someone coming and ran off. It was a postman.
>
> We both went and hid ourselves under a boiler hole at the Blue Button Colliery, close by. The postman looked in the direction of where she lay and then went on. We went away, but came back and saw Constable Jackson removing her body to the Anchor Inn in a trap.
>
> The night previous to the murder Davies was at our house. We were talking about Eliza. We agreed to meet her the next morning as she was going to work and kill her, no matter who she said she would have.
>
> I make this confession voluntarily as I cannot keep it any longer. I declare all I have stated to be true."

The police were delighted. At last the murder was solved. At the Stipendiary Magistrate's Court on Tuesday 28th July held before Mr Neville, Superintendent Walters read out Doughty's confession and applied for a week's remand until they could verify the details.

Mr Neville asked Doughty how he pleaded. He answered, "Mr Neville, I was brought before you on 11th May and discharged on 18th May. Some people are telling me I am going to the asylum. It is a lie what I have said. I know I have said it and I knew the wench, Eliza Cartwright well, but I never did it. It was not true."

The court was in uproar. Mr Neville had no option but to grant the police their week's remand in the hope that they could sort out the confusion. Doughty was removed to Stafford Goal to await a further court appearance.

So what exactly was happening? Why had Isaac Doughty walked all the way to Handsworth to confess to a crime which he afterwards denied?

Inquiries were to tell of a very troubled young man. Local opinions of Doughty were divided. Some believed that he was "unhinged" while others pointed to his intimate knowledge of the crime. The police discovered that he had been in trouble before and there had been a suggestion that he should be placed in an asylum.

Rumour had it that while "in his cups" he had tried to commit suicide. It was said that he had threatened to drown himself in the Pink Pool only to be rescued by two policemen who locked him up until he was sober.

That incident which happened about five years earlier had been followed by Doughty confessing to the same murder. On that occasion he had professed his innocence when he had sobered up and had been fined for wasting police time. It was true that he had been before Mr Neville on 11th May when he had been in trouble for drunkenness and was goaled for a week.

A sketch of Isaac Doughty in the Magistrates Court on 28th July 1896 by Express & Star artist, Goffin.

The most crucial discovery was that Doughty had lodged with Mrs Ball for six months before he made his first confession to the murder. That would obviously explain why he knew so much about the crime.

In an interview with the *Express & Star* Mrs Ball painted a very sad picture of her young lodger. Isaac's mother had died when he was very young and he had been reared by his grandmother, Mrs Harrison of Daisy Bank. His father had remarried and moved to live in Chell Street, though Isaac rarely lived with him, preferring to stay with his grandmother who idolised him. She had even kept him at school until he was 16, very rare in those days for people without much income.

During his childhood he was friends with Eliza, though nothing more because she was three years his senior. When his grandmother died he had moved from place to place and that was when he lodged with Mrs Ball. It would seem that it was around the same time that his peculiar behaviour began, but Mrs Ball never thought that he was mad, just "flighty" after a "cup of beer".

She told the reporter that never once had she suspected him of being responsible for her daughter's death, though she was amazed that "he should have his story so straight". Finally she remarked that she had no idea who the Davies man was. Doughty had never mentioned him to her and neither had Eliza.

With Davies the police drew a blank. Although they found a grave in Coseley churchyard belonging to one William Davies, no one could remember Doughty having any relationship with the man. Despite checking with all families with the same name in the area no one remembered Doughty.

For several weeks the police continued to investigate Doughty's background but were finally forced to conclude that he had made up the whole confession. On Tuesday 11th August 1896 before magistrates Tildesley and Broughall they applied for Doughty's release. With a severe warning as to his future behaviour, Isaac Doughty was discharged. Immediately afterwards he signed the pledge never to drink alcohol again.

Once more Eliza Cartwright's murder was placed in the unsolved files, where it remains to this day.

Solidly built Daisy Bank School still stands but is now a community centre and library.

Not Another Day in Birmingham
(Birmingham 1883 - B'ham Daily Gazette)

Sarah Davis was a pretty 17 year old who had left home shortly after her 15th birthday to work as a servant girl with Mr Muddyman who owned the Black Boy Stores in Jamaica Row, Birmingham. She worked less than a mile from her parents' home, but Sarah had to stay with the Muddyman family because her duties included lighting the fires in the early morning and helping the cook to prepare breakfast.

It seemed she was contented there because she stayed with the family for over eighteenth months, not once complaining about her job or her employer. Even so, an inquest would later show a secretive side to Sarah and that she may not have been quite as happy as everyone thought.

On the evening of 20th May 1883 she left the Black Boy Stores at about 7 o'clock. It was thought she was going to see her parents but instead she went into the town to meet her sweetheart, a market drover called William Emery. William was a surprise to everyone since no one had known about the lad. During the evening Sarah also met a friend, Emily Preston, and they chatted for a while.

At around 8.45 pm Sarah and William casually walked around the city centre until they reached the Birmingham and Fazeley Canal, where Sarah suddenly went into the water and, despite William's efforts, she drowned. William ran from the canal side but it was about 12.30am before he came upon Police Sergeant Shepherd in Great Barr Street. Blurting out that his girlfriend had jumped into the canal he took the officer back to the scene, but Sarah's body could not be found. It was not until two hours later that her corpse was dragged from the canal some 800 yards from where her parents lived and taken to the Moseley Street Mortuary.

Her death left many questions. Why would such a happy young girl drown herself? Why wait until she was with her sweetheart? Why did William not save her, after all, it was only a canal? Was it suicide or had William pushed her into the water then tried to make it look like suicide by fetching the police? Why had it taken the lad so long to find help? Was he making sure that Sarah was dead before he did so? Only an inquest and a trial might answer those questions.

Proceedings started later the same day before Stipendiary Magistrates Mr Kynnersley and Dr. Russell at the Public Office, Moor Street. Twenty one year old William Emery of 22 Court, 8 House, Barford Street was charged with causing the death of Sarah Davis. Only two people gave evidence.

THE SUSPECTED MURDER OF A SWEET-HEART IN BIRMINGHAM.

Sergeant Shepherd said that at about 12.30am on 21st May William Emery had met him in Great Barr Street and said that a young woman had jumped into the canal and drowned herself. The Sergeant had gone with the prisoner to the scene, which was on the arm of the canal between Garrison Lane and Saltley. Emery had said that the girl was his sweetheart and when she jumped into the water she pulled him in too. After a few minutes he got out but could not save the girl. She had struggled hard but went down screaming.

The Sergeant asked Emery to point out the exact spot and he had thrown a pebble into the canal. "Having procured a drag team, sir", the Sergeant continued, "it took us two hours to locate the body. We then removed it to the mortuary." During the drag operation the Sergeant asked two men working at a nearby brickyard whether they had heard any commotion during the drowning, but they had heard nothing.

The magistrates next questioned William about his behaviour on the fatal evening.

"Why did you not try to save the girl?" asked Mr. Kynnersley.
"I thought it was enough for one to be drowned at once," replied William.
"And why did you not seek help sooner?" continued Mr. Kynnersley, to which William made no reply.

Convinced that William's answers, or lack of them, were for some unsavoury reason, the magistrates remanded him in custody for the following week when further investigations would have been made and the medical report would be available for the inquest.

The inquest took place at the Public Office on 31st May 1883 before Mr. Henry Hawkes, the Borough Coroner.

The first witness was Mr. A Muddyman, Sarah's employer. He told the court that she had left his house after having her tea at about 7 o'clock on the evening of 20th May. She had told him that she was going to visit her parents at 129 Garrison Lane and he asked her to be back by 9 o'clock.

Mr Muddyman had been surprised to learn that Sarah had a boyfriend because she had never spoken of any young man. When he learned it was William Emery he supposed that they had met at his stores because William was often there. As to Sarah's character, Mr Muddyman said that she was "a steady, hard working, honest servant" and he had "not the slightest reason to suppose that she was likely to commit suicide".

Neither had the next witness, Emily Preston. She was also a servant and had been friends with Sarah since the previous Christmas, but, like Mr Muddyman, she knew nothing of the boyfriend. On the evening of 20th May she had left her home at 72 Great Barr Street and at 8.40 she had met Sarah with a young man in Bordesley. As they stopped to chat the young man walked on. They spoke for some time and at the end of their conversation Sarah had said, "Well, Emily, we have met for the last time."

"What did she mean by that?" asked the coroner.
"I thought that she was leaving town, sir, and asked her where she was going. She said, "You will soon know. I am not going to live in Birmingham another day." When I asked her where she was going that evening she said that she was going to visit her parents for the last time. She then wished me "Goodnight", sir, and we parted."

Emily Preston told the court that she thought Sarah was leaving the town, nothing else. However, she remembered Sarah saying in a previous conversation that her father had found her another job. She was angry and said that "rather than accept it she would go on tramp", that is, beg for money. As to Sarah's manner on the evening of 20th, Emily said that her friend seemed "perfectly sober and there was nothing unusual in her appearance".

So far none of the evidence suggested a reason for Sarah Davis to commit suicide. Had she been murdered by William Emery? When the surgeon, Dr. Barratt, gave his statement even that possibility seemed doubtful. He told the court that in the post mortem he had found Sarah Davis had been well nourished with all the internal organs healthy. All the signs on the body were "consistent with a death from suffocation by drowning" and there were no other marks of violence.

There remained the question of why William Emery did so very little to save the girl. He was asked if he wanted to make a statement to the court, and though he didn't have to say anything Emery was determined to be heard.

He told the court that he had left Jamaica Row with Sarah at about 8.40 on the fatal evening. She had given him some apples and nuts and they ate them as they walked about Bull Street and Dale End. They had walked as far as Moseley Road then sat for some time on a bench near Highgates Park. Later they walked down Bradford Street to the town and then along Lawley Street and Lander Street until they reached the canal.

Suddenly Sarah had said to him, "You go away. I am not going back home again." Then she had walked off along the canal towpath in the direction of Garrison Lane. He thought that she had been heading for her parents' home and so he followed, but without warning she jumped into the water.

William told the court that he caught hold of her arm to drag her out but she had pulled him into the canal. There the coroner interrupted.
"But your trousers were wet only to the fork."
"I could not swim, sir. She plunged into the middle of the canal before I could catch hold of her."
"Did you scramble out?" asked the coroner.
"Seeing I could not get hold of her I scrambled out," William admitted.
"Then you would stand in the narrow part of the canal and watch the poor girl drown?" asked the coroner.
"I could not swim, sir," pleaded the sorrowful William.
"Did you not cry out for help?" continued the coroner.
"No, sir, there was no one about."
"You knew there were some brick huts near at hand."
"I didn't know, sir," said William.

He went on to tell the court how he eventually found Sergeant Shepherd and took him back to the canal.

It was William's lack of action which led the jury to think he might not be telling the full truth. They decided that "Sarah Davis had come to her death by drowning, but there was not sufficient evidence at that time to show how she got into the canal". The coroner remanded William Emery into custody charged with having caused the girl's death pending further investigations.

On 1st June William appeared in the court again before Mr. Kynnersley. He had been charged with murdering Sarah Davis, but the police had no further evidence to offer and reported that they had little hope of ever getting any more. The magistrate released Emery, but added, "you did not seem to have been at the slightest pains or to have made any effort to save the life of the poor girl. It is a most disgraceful thing".

Highway Robbery
(Birmingham 1817 -Aris's B'ham Gazette)

In the early 19th nineteenth century travel by road was dangerous. Main roads were largely to a good turnpike standard but lesser ways could do you serious harm. If not, then footpads lurked behind every bush and bend, particularly if you travelled alone. Some unfortunate people could not avoid these dangers because their living depended upon travelling. Such was the case of Mr Pennington.

Seven o'clock on the evening of Thursday 6th February 1817 had seen him complete his business in Birmingham and so he set off in his gig (a small horse drawn carriage) towards his next call in Castle Bromwich.

Some time after 8 o'clock that night two passers-by found his body lying at the roadside between Vauxhall Gardens and the village of Saltley. Barely alive, he was taken to a nearby tollhouse but died soon afterwards without giving any clues about his attackers.

At 9.30 the corpse was moved to Vauxhall Infirmary where examination showed that the poor man had been shot through the head after a struggle. Presumably he had been stopped for his money and when he refused to hand it over was dragged from his gig and shot. His belongings showed that his name was Pennington of the wine merchants, Pennington and Bell-Chambers of London, so they were told of the tragedy.

When the inquest opened at Vauxhall on Monday 10th February the police had very little to act upon save for the fact that Mr Pennington had probably lost some of his property which might be traced. News travelled very slowly in those days and the court had not yet heard from the dead man's partner. Mr Whateley, the coroner, did his best to discover more about the circumstances but there were few details. Even the newspapers did not think it worth reporting much about the inquest.

A doctor (not named) gave post mortem evidence that Mr Pennington had been shot while still in his gig and then dragged to the ground. A ball had passed through the lower part of the back of his head and lodged inside. There was no other signs of violence. Only the clothing seemed ruffled, caused when the body was dragged to the ground.

Birmingham wine merchants who were friends of the dead man told the court that when they went to identify the body they discovered that he had been robbed of a gold watch and some cash. Even so, most of the things he had with him had escaped the villains. Mr Pennington was around 50 years old and left a pregnant wife and seven small children.

The only other witnesses (also not named) were the two men who discovered the body, but they could add nothing to their bare description of how they had come across the corpse.

In view of the lack of evidence Mr Whateley instructed the jury to returned a verdict of "Wilful murder against person or persons unknown", which they did. Closing the hearing, he wished the police rapid success in catching the killer, or killers.

The High Constable of Birmingham, William Payne, posted a reward of 100 guineas for "any person or persons whose information should lead to the apprehension and conviction of the perpetrators of this barbarous deed". The notice went on: "should either of the parties concerned (excepting the person by whom the pistol was fired) impeach his accomplice, he will be entitled to the reward and every exertion will be made to obtain his pardon." [A guinea was £1-1sh and there were 20 shillings to the pound, so the offer was £105.]

So enraged were the local guardians of the law that on 9th February the Churchwardens and Overseers of the Poor of the Parish of Aston offered a further 50 guineas. This made a total of £157-10sh, a great amount of money which should have brought up some information, but strangely no one seemed to have anything to say.

On 24th February High Constable Payne received a letter from a friend of Pennington which gave descriptions of two stolen items. The gold watch was distinctive because of the inscription "Ellicott, Royal Exchange" on the inside. A missing purse was described as long and green with slides to separate bank notes. It had held some guineas and 7 one shilling pieces [35p] when Mr Pennington left London. The friend thought it most unlikely that the dead man had spent it all because he was on a selling tour and not collecting money owed.

In the same week the High Constable received a letter from the Reverend D Wood of Rugby. A man named Gardner, he wrote, had confessed to the murder and implicated two brothers named Hiorn. Immediately Payne dispatched a constable from Brinklow to Rugby to apprehend the men. However, when they were brought to Birmingham and questioned it soon became obvious that the confession was false.

Gardner admitted immediately that he had been induced to make the confession by a man named Fox who hoped to claim the rewards. That man could not be found, but William Payne questioned one of the Hiorn brothers. It soon became clear that he too had nothing to do with the murder because of clear evidence that he and his brother were 26 miles away from Birmingham at 5 o'clock on the evening of the crime. In those days it would have been impossible to cover such a distance before 8 o'clock when the body was found.

Questioned further, Gardner admitted that he had made up the whole story and had never in his entire life visited Birmingham. In fact the closest he had ever been was some 10 miles away. Thoroughly annoyed, High Constable Payne arrested Gardner for wasting police time and he was kept in custody to appear at the next Warwick Assizes. At that trial in late March it emerged that as a reward for his confession the Reverend Wood had given Thomas Gardner a silver watch. That made his offence the more serious and he was sentenced to a year in goal for fraud.

The police continued to investigate and even secured help from that debauched voluptuary, the Prince Regent. The future George IV effectively held the royal reins during George III's frequent bouts of insanity and arranged a royal pardon. It was offered to any of the criminals who gave information leading to capture of the killer except for the one who fired the shot. And the Prince Regent himself offered a reward of 150 guineas for the capture and conviction of the murderer, though how he would have paid it in view of his colossal gambling debts was not explained.

By the end of February 1817 no less than 300 guineas reward was on offer [£315] but it made no difference. The police reasoned that any accomplice would surely grab the reward and take his chances, especially with a royal pardon in view, so most likely the crime was committed by one man. At all events, no murderer was ever found.

A Victim of Charity
(Hanford 1877 - Daily Sentinel)

Martha Sillitoe had lived in the quiet potteries village of Hanford between Stoke and Trentham for most of her life. She had married the village butcher in the 1820s and reared two sons. After her husband's death in the 1840s and the death of both sons she had sold the business and moved to a small cottage near the police station. There she lived happily, preferring her own company, until the night of 19th December 1877.

On the afternoon of the 20th neighbours realised they had not seen the 78 year old all day and persuaded the local constable to enter her cottage. The front door was closed but not locked, and inside they found Martha Sillitoe lying at the foot of the stairs. The pool of blood suggested that she had not just fallen.

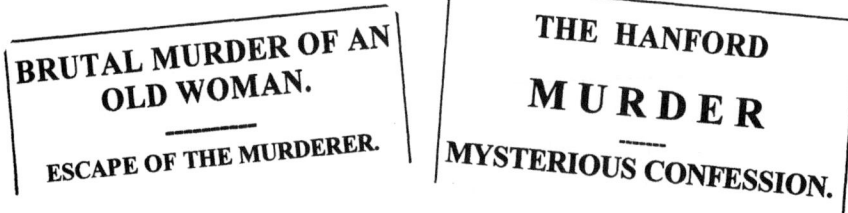

When the inquest opened at the Bull's Head Inn on Monday 24th December under Mr Booth witnesses described the old lady's unusual and secluded life. Although Martha took an active part in church affairs she rarely socialised with the villagers and even her next door neighbour, Mrs Perrins, rarely saw her.

Mrs Perrins told the hearing that Martha might go for days without being seen, but she had spoken to her on Wednesday 19th December when the old lady had brought a present for the Perrins's children. During that visit Martha had told her neighbour that she would be very busy the following week as she was expecting friends to stay. She had not revealed their names.

On leaving Martha had made it perfectly clear that she was going to church that evening. It was her absence from church and the fact that none of her window shutters were open the next day which led Mrs Perrins to seek the constable at about 3 o'clock on Thursday afternoon. Mrs Perrins also revealed that the old lady was in the habit of employing tramps to do odd jobs around her house, like getting in coal or chopping firewood, for which she would give food or a little money.

Constable Smith's station was only two doors from the cottage. He had found Martha Sillitoe lying on her back at the foot of the stairs in a pool of blood. She had several deep wounds about the head, possibly caused by a flat iron found close by. Her nose and one eye were severely bruised as though someone had punched her. Finally he discovered two stab wounds in her throat which had punctured the windpipe. As the corpse was cold and stiff he presumed that the crime had been committed the evening before.

Further police investigations at the cottage suggested that a likely motive for the murder was theft. In the bedroom PC Smith had found unlocked drawers pulled out and their contents scattered over the floor. Locked drawers had been left untouched. On the stairs he had found a purse, a bunch of keys and a candlestick. He also noticed footprints made when the killer had got blood on the soles of his shoes before going up the stairs.

With no other evidence available at that stage the coroner, Mr Booth, adjourned the inquest telling the police he hoped for a speedy solution to the horrific crime. They had one positive lead to help them, said the coroner. Mrs Sillitoe's charity towards tramps had "surely cost her life". Could they trace any callers at her cottage before they melted away? Not so much a lead, you might think, as the coroner's general distaste for poor, scruffy, uneducated people, but would it help solve the murder?

There had been a young man around Hanford village on Wednesday, 19th December. Ostensibly he had been hawking brushes, though he was carrying only one. Neighbours thought he might have sold it to Martha Sillitoe because the man had been to several houses trying to change a shilling piece for the "old lady at the cottage". He eventually got change at the post office. Villagers described him as young and "better dressed than the usual tramps seen about the village", and they remembered his long coat.

Some children passing the cottage at around 10 o'clock on the Wednesday evening had seen a young man coming down the cottage stairs. Being children they had thought nothing of it and so told no one.

Those pieces of information convinced the police that the hawker was their man and for weeks they visited all the lodging houses and other places frequented by tramps and their like in the Potteries area. Their search was unsuccessful; the hawker had simply disappeared.

One of the difficulties the police had to contend with was not knowing exactly what had been stolen from the cottage. Villagers knew that Mrs

Sillitoe was quite well off but she had rarely displayed her wealth. They were pretty certain that clothing and a silver watch were missing but could give only scanty descriptions.

With few accurate details all the police could hope for was that pawnbrokers would report any strange men trying to pawn female belongings. Nothing emerged and investigations seemed to be reaching stalemate when two separate arrests brought new hope.

The first to be arrested was William Fairbanks, alias "Pottery Jack", who was taken into custody at Church Acton in late December on suspicion of burglary in the Penkridge area. A native of Spot Gate, Longton, he was well known for his criminal activities and was wanted by Staffordshire Police for several burglaries around Longton. On 31st December 1877 he went before the Penkridge Magistrates and was remanded in custody for further questioning.

Fairbanks was asked about his whereabouts in 19th December. He seemed to have a good alibi, but as he fitted the description of the wanted hawker the police asked Hanford villagers to help them. None of them identified Fairbanks as the hawker and the police gave him up as a possible suspect.

The second man arrested seemed more likely to commit burglary and murder. George Shaw, alias John King and Pottery George, was arrested at Coseley near Wolverhampton on 17th January 1878 for breaking into a house and trying to steal clothing. He was disturbed by the owner and there was a struggle in which Shaw had drawn a knife, but had been overpowered.

Shaw was notorious as a dangerous and habitual criminal who had only been released from a seven year sentence for violent crimes in October 1877. Superintendent Wollaston from Brierley Hill and Chief Detective Hackney of Stafford became suspicious that Shaw might be involved in several murders, including that of Mrs Sillitoe.

Between the evening of 7th January and the morning of the 8th, Samuel Bowater, owner of the New British Iron and Coal company and the Black Wagon Colliery, was murdered when his home in Old Hill, Blackheath was burgled. Inquiries proved that Shaw was close to the district on 7th January being involved in a street brawl just a few miles away at Tipton. During that fight he had stabbed a man, though not fatally.

Convinced that Shaw could have killed Bowater and Mrs Sillitoe, the two detectives visited him in jail the following day. He had a head wound and his clothes were blood stained. Unable to give a satisfactory explanation for either and being evasive as to his whereabouts on 7th January they charged him with the murder of Bowater, but held back on the Hanford crime.

The following day Detective Hackney followed up on the Hanford case, visiting Shaw alone and questioning him further. Aware then that he might be accused of both crimes, Shaw began to relate a catalogue of crimes that he had committed in the Black Country at the relevant time to show that he could not have been in the Potteries

The first that he admitted, and offered as proof that he could not have killed Bowater, was the robbery of a house in the Tividale area on the night of that murder. Shaw gave Hackney the address and a list of the stolen property which when checked proved correct. In fact Shaw was wearing some of the articles when Hackney saw him.

Even so, the police were still not thoroughly convinced because Old Hill is barely 3 miles from Tividale. To prove his innocence Shaw went on to admit many more crimes, supplying both dates and lists of stolen items. Burglaries at Great Barr, West Bromwich, Tipton and Wolverhampton were checked and all the confessions proved correct.

Shaw gave the police dates and lists but he also told the police about pawnbrokers where he exchanged the goods for cash. When checking one such shop in Dudley the detectives were amazed at Shaw's guile and cheek.

While Hackney was interviewing the owner, Mr Hollins, he accidentally pulled from his pocket a pair of knitted cuffs he had taken from Shaw. Hollins immediately recognised them as part of some property stolen when his own shop had been burgled.

Confronting Shaw with the offence, Hackney got the distinct impression that Shaw enjoyed talking about his crimes. He told Hackney that he "had a good time of it" in the Hollins's shop. He had emptied a decanter of sherry, obtained a bottle of gin and was about to help himself to a round of beef when had had been disturbed and had to make a speedy exit. He might have been pleased but the Hollins's were not. Their prize dalmatian dog died the next day, probably from poisoning. Had Shaw poisoned it to make his robbery safer? He did not admit to that.

After confessing to another burglary at a pub in Cinder Bank, Dudley on 8th December, Shaw related how he had moved to the north of Staffordshire to continue his crimes. It was because of that that the police decided to move him to the Potteries for further questioning.

There he admitted to breaking into the house of a Mr Bettany at Stych in the Burslem area. He had had a narrow escape because he only just managed to climb through a window before the owner caught him. He had left behind a muffler, a cap and one of his boots.

From Burslem he had gone to Tunstall where he burgled the shop of a man named Stringer, stealing clothing and money. Then, having left his mark on the Potteries, he moved to the Stafford area. That being so the police moved him again - to Stafford.

Shaw told the Stafford Police that in early January 1878 he had burgled a house at New Town. While there he helped himself to a good meal before stealing money. Before leaving the house he wrote a note on a piece of paper which he left, strangely, covering a gold ring. "I starve with hunger; be satisfied. I don't want them.", meaning the ring.

Was Shaw getting a conscience? It seems unlikely because the same night he burgled a house in Stafford and helped himself to money from a bedroom. He would certainly have taken more but was interrupted by the owners.

Despite all the confessions, police were still convinced that he was responsible for Martha Sillitoe's death and charged him with the crime. He hotly disputed that and maintained that on the evening of 19th December he had been in Leek. Police could find no witnesses to corroborate his story, but, luckily for Shaw, could find none to place him anywhere near Hanford either. Eventually they had to drop the charge.

Shaw was undoubtedly a violent criminal "which even the annals of the Old Bailey could scarcely produce", as one *Daily Sentinel* reporter wrote, but he had never been convicted of murder. Often, instead of attacking the house or shop owner he had fled, and it was that sort of action which had led to his arrest in Coseley when the owner caught him and Shaw offered no resistance.

It seemed as though the death of Martha Sillitoe was going to remain a mystery, but there was one last curious chapter to the story.

Six and a half years later on 30th July 1884 a group of four boys were playing near the River Trent by Manor Farm at the bottom of Bavelcok Street, Stoke. There they came across a bottle lodged in the weeds inside which was a message which they immediately took to the police.

Written in red ink, it started with an explanation to the family of A Capewell that he had written the message and would insert it into a bottle. It would be thrown into the river near Bucknell Water Wheel so as not be found too soon and allow him time to drown without being rescued. The letter went on:

> "Confession before I drown myself and preparatory to meeting my Maker. I, A, Capewell, do confess that owing to my disgrace in having to leave my work at Bradbury's, and also that my daughter (cripple Eliza) is in the family way, if this should meet the eyes of anybody, kindly convey it to my widow and the police station and tell them that my terror-stricken conscience impels me to confess to the murder of the poor woman Sillitoe at Hanford, some years ago for gain."

Delighted that they might at last be able to close the file on Martha Sillitoe's murder, the police began to investigate Capewell's background. They soon found his family because he had been on police files since 9th July 1884 when Mrs Capewell reported him missing.

Albert Capewell had been a labourer who for the previous twelve years had lived at Grant Street, Stoke where his wife kept a general shop. For a time after coming to the Potteries he had worked for Mr Cooke at Manor Farm, but about two years before the bottle message was found he had worked for Bradbury's, furniture dealers. They said that he was a man of excellent character, temperate and quiet of habits. His wife added that he was subject to fits of depression which led him to disappear from home from time to time. That accounted for her not reporting his disappearance immediately.

She also told Stoke Police that a body had been found in the North Stafford Canal at Meaford, near Stone, on 11th July which she had identified as her husband. It had been difficult because when she had arrived at Stone the corpse had already been buried along with most of its clothes. Fortunately they had kept the boots, which she readily identified. She had also taken with her a daguerreotype, an early form of photograph, which people who had seen the corpse recognised as the drowned man. To save further embarrassment Mrs Capewell had not insisted that the body be exhumed.

[The only canal at Meaford is and has always been the Trent & Mersey, but "North Stafford " might have been a local name.]

Investigations seemed to be going well for the Stoke Police, but when they examined several documents written by Capewell who, "although no scholar, wrote a hand which was not without its distinguishing characteristics", it became clear that "the communication found in the bottle was never written by the same hand".

River experts also insisted that if the bottle had been thrown in the river at the Bucknall Water Wheel, the place where Capewell had confessed in his letter to having thrown it in, then it would have had to negotiate numerous weirs and other obstructions and could not have reached the place where the boys found it. They also concluded that it was strange that it was located "in a spot within a few yards of his residence".

Further investigations showed that Capewell rarely missed work at Fenton Farm, where he worked when the murder happened, leaving home early in the morning and returning at 6 o'clock in the evening. The police concluded that the confession was nothing more than a "cruel hoax" by some unknown person.

But why would anyone try to fasten this *particular* six and a half year old murder on Capewell if the forger had no interest except in a hoax? Had the real murderer spotted the drowned body of Capewell and seized an opportunity to lay the blame elsewhere. And then, Stoke is only about two miles from Hanford.

A Cap for Little Willie
(Deepfields 1892 - Express & Star)

There was nothing unusual about the morning of 6th January 1892 at the Barrett household except for a light fall of snow. John Barrett was up early and left the house in Anchor Yard to head for his work as a fireman at the Spring Vale Steelworks in Deepfields. As usual he ate no breakfast because his young son would carry it to the works between 8.30 and 9.00. There he would wait until his father was finished then take the empty "snapping tin" home and head off to school.

The lad's route to and from the steelworks was about 1,100 yards along the towpath of the Birmingham Canal, and on that morning he left his father and headed home at 8.50 am. He never arrived and two days later, as his father looked on, his naked body was dragged from the canal at Ten Score Bridge, Deepfields.

The police might have recorded another sad case of drowning, but John Barrett insisted that his son would never go swimming in the canal on such a cold morning. John was also adamant that the coat his son wore was impossible for the lad to get off without help because it fitted so tightly. The police were forced to agree that it seemed to be a case of murder.

MYSTERIOUS DROWNING FATALITY AT DEEPFIELDS.

By 11th January when the inquest took place at the Anchor Inn, Deepfields, preliminary investigations had found several men who were near the canal on the fatal morning. Enoch Fellows, a miner, said that he had seen the boy coming from the direction of the Spring Vale Steelworks at around 9 o'clock. He was wearing a topcoat and a tippet [cap] and was seen about 100 yards from where the body was found.

Another miner, Benjamin Flowers, said that he had seen a canal boat coming from Oldbury towards Wolverhampton when the boat's steerer called out to him. He had asked if Flowers had seen a lad walking along the towpath carrying "snappings". Flowers said that he had seen no one to which the steerer replied, "I have just found a cap, a can and some snappings". He didn't know the name of the boatman.

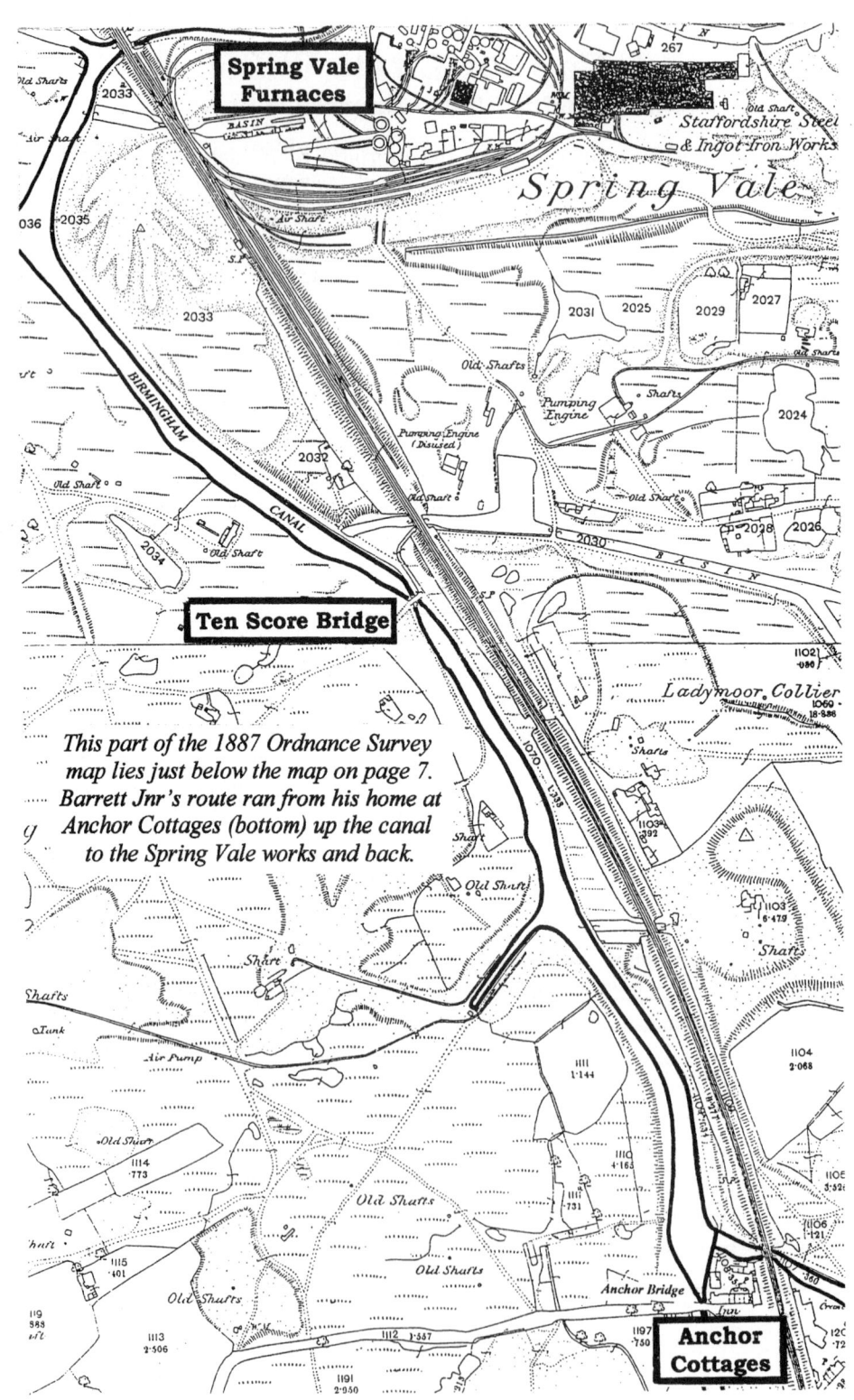

This part of the 1887 Ordnance Survey map lies just below the map on page 7. Barrett Jnr's route ran from his home at Anchor Cottages (bottom) up the canal to the Spring Vale works and back.

Despite his obvious distress, John Barrett told the hearing that his son had left him at 8.50 with his coat buttoned up because it was very cold. He did not think for one moment that the lad would try to remove the coat himself and the coroner agreed. Curiously, he told the court that weeks beforehand his son had lost £1-3s-6d [£1.17½], a lot of money in those days, and a breakfast can when a boatman had snatched them from him as he walked home along the canal. Unfortunately John Barrett had not told the police.

The only other witness was Dr Baker, the surgeon who had made a preliminary examination of the body. All that he could say so far was that the boy had died from drowning. The coroner ordered a full post mortem and adjourned the inquest.

The police circulated descriptions of the boy's possessions in the local newspapers. The can would be easily recognised as it bore the inscription "H. Delaney, Bilston" on a brass plate and the cap had a badge with the motto "Play Up". A reward was offered for their recovery in the hope that someone had just found and kept them.

It was not until 19th January that the landlord of the Navigation Inn in Engine Street, Tat Bank, Oldbury reported to the police that some time ago one of his customers, Jeremiah Edwards, had bragged of finding a boy's overcoat and cap near the Birmingham Canal on the day of the murder.

On Saturday 23rd Inspector Bishop, Superintendent Speke and Detective Moreton interviewed Edwards, a boatman, at his home in Engine Street next to the Navigation Inn. Foolishly Edwards denied ever having seen the articles mentioned and also denied being near Deepfields for at least two months. Unconvinced, the officers returned on 25th January and Edwards changed his story. He had made a dreadful mistake, he said, and forgotten that he had been at Deepfields on the day of the crime. He also admitted finding a cap on his boat, the *Jackson*, when he was near Coseley Tunnel. During that interview he gave them the name of his steerer, Richard Williams.

On 26th January Constable Bayliss interviewed Williams in Chapel Street, Tividale. Like his partner, he denied finding anything on 6th January though he did admit to being on the canal that day near Ten Score Bridge. Refusing to believe this, the police saw him again on 6th February when he admitted that he and Edwards had taken the clothes. When he heard of the murder he had dumped the coat in the canal at Dudley Port (it was later recovered) but Edwards had kept the cap and later that day (6th January) had given it to a relation. Further implicating his partner, Williams said that it was Edwards who had found the articles and given him the coat for a shilling [5p].

The police were convinced that they had their murderers and arrested both men. On Monday 8th February Edwards and Williams were charged at Bilston Police Station before a magistrate, Mr T Holcroft, with the murder of John Willie Barrett. A second charge was brought of stealing a coat, cap and breakfast things, the property of John Barrett.

Inspector Bishop, stationed at Old Hill, described how he, Constable Moreton and Superintendent Speke had interviewed Williams about the missing articles. He had warned Williams not to lie because it would be used against him in court.

Williams had replied, "Well, I will tell you the truth from the bottom of my heart. I pulled the things out of the cut canal and put them on the boat. Jerry (Edwards) had the cans and the cap: I had a can and coat. I put them in the cut at Dudley Port. It was a little blue coat with a cape on. I said to Jerry, I shall give information and he said, "No, we will take them home. We shall get into bother if we leave them now." Then he turned round and hooted at me and said I should have more sense than feel [ie have feelings]. We should be on the inquest and lose a day's pay."

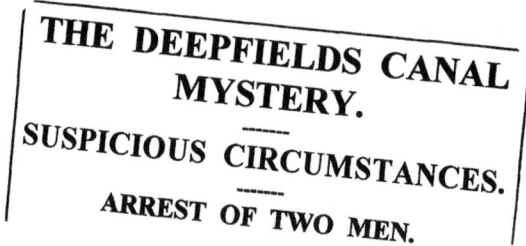

Having got that statement from Williams, Edwards was arrested at the Navigation Inn. He was very drunk and could not understand what was happening, so they left the charge until he had sobered up. The following morning Inspector Bishop read out Williams' statement in front of both men.

Edwards said, "I have got my chance now. We were gong along the Deepfields cut, sometimes I would see him (Williams) and sometimes not." The Inspector explained to the magistrate that it was snowing at the time. "I saw him reaching things out of the cut. I asked him what they were and he said, "There's a cap, a can, a coat and some saucers." I said that he had better stop the horse [towing the boat] and fetch a policeman."

"I hooted to some men who were sinking a pit near Ten Score Bridge and asked them if they had seen anyone with breakfast things. They said they hadn't and upon that Williams said, "We will take them home and make a drink."

Inspector Harrison told the court that Williams had said he had the coat but sunk it near Mr Holcroft's Works at Tividale and would point out the spot, which he later did. [The works had the same name as the magistrate hearing the case, but we don't know if there was any connection.] Edwards had taken the cap, but gave it to one of his relations with some tin saucers.

So far the police had not interviewed the relations of Edwards and Williams and the Inspector asked the court for more time to investigate. Mr Holcroft asked them if they had anything more to add, to which they both said, "No", claiming their innocence, and he remanded them in custody.

On 23rd February Williams and Edwards appeared before other magistrates, Mr H Ward and Mr R Clayton, where the police sought committal for trial at the Assizes. From the outset there was no problem in proving that the two prisoners had obtained young John Barrett's possessions dishonestly, the difficulty was to show how they came by them.

Dr Isaiah Baker gave the post mortem evidence. During the examination on 11th January he had discovered no marks of violence on the boy's body. The cause of death was asphyxia from drowning. The corpse contained a lot of water in the stomach and a certain amount of frothy fluid in the lungs. In his opinion if the two prisoners had tried to take off the coat while the boy was still alive then they would most certainly have caused physical damage. Dr Baker had therefore ruled out violence and raised a string of questions as to how and why the boy had ended naked in the canal.

The next witness was Mr Cook, a storekeeper at Jones Brothers Galvanising Works, who met the two men as they delivered their cargo of acid at around 11.45 on 6th January. Both men, he said, appeared relaxed and he could see nothing strange in their behaviour.

A Mrs Tolley also spoke of their relaxed attitude. She lived by the canal at Oldbury and between 4 and 5 o'clock on 6th January the two men passed in their boat. Edwards, her brother in law, threw her a cap shouting "Here's an old hat for little Willie!" She picked it up and said, "It looks rather crummy", and was about to throw it into the canal when her son, Willie, took it from her. A fortnight later Edwards had appeared wanting the cap back, but her son had lost it. Edwards said, "They are after me for that old cap", and looked shocked that it was lost.

Eliza Lloyd was Mrs Tolley's neighbour and was with Mrs Tolley when Edwards threw her the cap. She remembered him saying that he had also found a topcoat, breakfast can and saucers, but she too was adamant that Edwards was perfectly happy.

Willie Tolley told the court that he had taken the cap with him that same day and gone sliding on the ice. Unfortunately he had tumbled into the pool and lost the cap.

The last two witness were Thomas Croft Rogers, landlord of the Navigation Inn, Tat Bank, Oldbury and his wife, and both told identical stories. On the night of 6th January Edwards had visited the pub and told him, "Me and my mate have had a good day today. We have found a lad's coat, cap and can in the cut at Deepfields. We went on and hurried through the stop in case we might be collared." Rogers told the court, that Edwards did not seem worried about his story.

However, on 18th January Mrs Rogers read a report of the inquest in the *Express & Star* and when Edwards came to the pub that evening she called him into the sitting room and said, "Jerry, there is an account of an inquest at Deepfields where a lad lost his overcoat." Edwards did not say anything and so Mrs Rogers read the account to him (Edwards could not read) then said, "If I were you I would take the things back to the police."

Later that week Mrs Rogers had seen the police advertisement in the *Express & Star* asking for sightings of the missing articles and once more she approached Edwards. "Go and take the things back" she said, "and say that you're no scholar and that a publican's wife read it to you." The prisoner did not say anything to her but as he walked up the passage she heard him say, "If the ----- want it let them find it." She added that Edwards had given her one of the saucers but she had returned it.

The canal behind Engine St is now a green and pleasant walk.

It was that behaviour which worried the couple and so they had told the police who went to interview Edwards on 23rd January. And it was that behaviour which led the magistrates to believe that Edwards and Williams were hiding some dark secret when they committed them for trial at Stafford.

On 29th March 1892 they appeared before Mr Justice Hawkins on charges of murdering John Willie Barrett and stealing the clothing and other belongings of John Barrett.

Mr Plumtre for the prosecution summarised the events of the morning of 6th January but had to admit that although the prisoners' statements were full of suspicion, he had no direct evidence that the prisoners ever saw the little lad alive, or had thrown him into the water.

With that admission the judge stopped the trial and directed the jury to find both prisoners not guilty of murder. Before the second charge was considered the judge lectured both men for obstructing the police investigation. Their appearance in his court, he said, was due to their own stupid behaviour and as they had both admitted taking the articles he would sentence them the following day. Mr Justice Hawkins probably wanted to teach Edwards and Williams a lesson by keeping them in prison overnight, because the next day he only fined them.

Williams and Edwards might breathe a sigh of relief, but due to their misdirected investigations the police still had a murder on their hands. The time spent gathering evidence against these two allowed the real murderer to get away and he never was found.

It left the questions of who removed John Willie Barret's tight coat, how did he get into the canal given that there was no sign of violence, and was there any connection between the death and the boatman who had stolen the boy's money and snap tin shortly before the murder?

Bearing False Witness
(Birmingham 1834 – Aris's B'ham Gazette)

A survey by students and professors of Warwick University in early 2002 concluded that money is the greatest asset in providing happiness. Unfortunately, as the police will tell you, it is also the greatest cause of crime. Imagine then a situation when the authorities dangle money around to persuade people to come forward to identify a criminal. Rewards are not common today but in the early 19th century when the police force barely existed they were often used to find witnesses.

Samuel Webb and his wife lived in Lawley Street, Birmingham and by 1834 both were in their early 60s. Though not well off, they had money put aside for their old age. To make life easier for themselves they were both still working. Samuel had his allotment in Green Lanes where he grew vegetables and raised pigs, and his wife worked from home preparing and selling the produce. Every morning Samuel would set off to his allotment and at 4.00 pm Mrs Webb would take him his tea. And so it had been for years since the end of Samuel's army days, when he had lost an eye in Egypt. The Chelsea Pension he received for his injury could not keep them adequately, but the allotment allowed them to be self sufficient. It was a hard life, but happy.

On Wednesday 10th April 1834 Samuel left home for his allotment as usual and Mrs Webb (we don't know her first name) left the house that afternoon to go to the baker's for pikelets or cakes. By 3 o'clock she had returned and must have started to prepare tea as usual. At 3.30 pm a little girl named Sarah Divett from the same block of terraced houses was playing outside the Webb's house. She chanced to look through the open kitchen door and saw Mrs Webb sprawled across the kitchen floor with blood everywhere.

Sarah's scream summoned the neighbours and there was pandemonium in the alleyway until the local constable arrived. When they examined the body they found that Mrs Webb's throat had been cut and there was a deep wound on the side of her head. The coat and shawl she had probably worn on the shopping trip had been thrown over the corpse in an attempt to hide it. In her hand they discovered a knife. Had Mrs Webb committed suicide?

A thorough search of the house showed that a box kept upstairs had been rummaged through, suggesting that the motive for the crime was theft. Samuel Webb had quickly been summoned from his allotment and told the officers that it had contained 46 silver shillings. They had been kept in a pocket book which was missing, but the thief must have been disturbed because the box still contained an old petticoat in which were wrapped twenty gold sovereigns.

If the thief had been disturbed how had he or she escaped without being seen? Unfortunately the Webb's house, unlike the others, had a second door in the side alley which the killer could have used. The police questioned little Sarah but she had seen no one unusual in the street that afternoon.

When the inquest opened on Saturday 13th at the Globe Tavern in Vauxhall Row virtually nothing else had been discovered. All that was clear was that Mrs Webb had died quickly and very cruelly.

Mr Wood who performed the post mortem told the hearing that the deep wound in the woman's throat had divided the carotoid artery and jugular vein causing severe loss of blood. He had also found a contused wound on the outside of the head as if a hammer blow had penetrated the skull.

"And what of the knife in the deceased's left hand?" asked Mr Whateley, the coroner.
"No doubt it was placed there by the murderer," replied Mr Wood, "in a vain attempt to suggest suicide."
"And why could it not have been suicide?" continued the coroner.
"Firstly, sir, Mrs Webb was right handed and secondly, there was no blood on her hand. One would have expected blood everywhere, especially on the hand. And finally, there was only one small spot on the actual knife."

Mr Wood told the hearing that in his opinion Mrs Webb had been knocked to the floor by the blow on the head and her throat had been cut to stop her shouting for help. The murderer must have had blood on his or her clothing.

But who might the killer be? Who would know that the Webbs had money in the house? A stranger who kept a lookout was unlikely, but neighbours knew everything about one another. Could Lawley Street be harbouring the murderer? Mr Whateley was determined to flush out the culprit and offered a £50 reward.

[It is very difficult to compare the value of money in 1834 with that in 2002, but here goes. Charles Dickens published *A Christmas Carol* in 1846 and from that we know that Ebeneezer Scrooge paid his clerk, Bob Cratchit, 30 shillings a year, which we would now call £1.50, a wage of 3p per week.]

Rewards were popular at the time because the constables were not regular, paid officers and had little time to investigate every story. Many witnesses had to be taken at their word, and the word was that John Fitter, shoemaker, who lived next door but one to the Webbs, was the murderer.

The constables had no option but to question John Fitter and to search his home. Naturally he denied everything, but upstairs in the garret they discovered an old, red soldier's jacket which, strangely, had the sleeve linings missing. Then they found his leather cobbler's apron with some of the leather shaved off, as if the owner had been trying to remove something, and a pair of trousers with spots of blood on them.

Questioned by the coroner, Fitter said that the apron had been stained when he had sold six wax plasters to a man who had cut his finger. He had tried to put one of the plasters on the wound and blood had dripped onto his apron. As to the blood on his trousers, he said that had happened when he had helped a neighbour kill a pig a week ago. In those days it was impossible to distinguish human from animal blood, but Fitter's stories could be checked.

It emerged that he had indeed helped to kill a neighbour's pig and had sold plasters to the man with a cut finger, but could these incidents have been used as cover for his crime? Undecided, the constables searched his house again. This time they discovered a pair of pincers used to take nails from shoes with tell tale signs of blood. Despite his protests, John Fitter was arrested and charged with the murder of Mrs Webb.

On Monday 11th August 1834 his trial began at Warwick Assizes, but from the outset the prosecution was in difficulty. Offering rewards produced witnesses whose truthfulness was always suspect.

First to give evidence was Mary Hudson. She did not live in the area but had gone to the authorities with her story. She had been, she said, in Lawley

Street between 3 and 4 o'clock on 10th April and was about to knock on Mrs Webb's door to ask if she could use the toilet. Looking through the window to see if there was anyone about, she had seen John Fitter standing over a body. He seemed to be holding the woman's head in his right arm as if to stop it hitting the floor. Presuming that the man was the husband and that he was helping his wife who might have had a fit, Mary Hudson told the court that she walked away so as not to disturb the couple. It was only when she heard of the murder that she went to the authorities.

Highly suspicious of her motives for coming forward, counsel for the defence asked why she had not appeared at the coroner's inquest.

"Because I did not know of the murder then," Mary replied.
"Or of the reward," asked the advocate sarcastically.

He accused her directly of coming forward only for the money, but she denied it. Even when confronted with evidence that she had spoken to two local women about the crime before she came forward she denied those conversations. And when asked why the police could not find anyone in the area who had seen her or whose house she had called at to use their lavatory on the fatal day, Mary Hudson just said that she had been in Lawley Street but had gone "up another entry".

Next came the "evidence" of Mary Ann Pattison, a soldier's widow, who swore that she had gone to Fitter's home at about 3.30 p.m. on 10th April to have a pair of boots repaired. When she arrived he was not there but had come back some three or four minutes later. Despite her attempts to stop him he had ignored her and gone straight through the kitchen and into the cellar. She told the court that she distinctly remembered that he had opened the cellar door with his left hand but had closed it later with his right. It was as if he was hiding his right hand lest she should see it, but she clearly saw that he had blood on his left hand.

At the time that Fitter entered he was wearing his red jacket, a cap, apron and slippers. However, before she had time to shout to him another man came in and went upstairs to the workshop. That must have disturbed Fitter because he came up from the cellar. He was not wearing his jacket and apron but he still had blood on his hands.

"What did you do then?" asked the prosecutor.
"I asked him to mend the boots," replied Mary Pattison, "but he seemed very bothered and said, 'Not now, my girl. I cannot just now,' and so I left and

went to Mrs Rufford's to speak about some washing." (Mary Pattison seems to have earned a living by taking in washing.) "While there I also spoke to Mrs Rufford about some cups and bowls from Mrs Dearns."

Questioned about the times and conversations she had had, Mary Pattison was adamant that she had told the truth and so was excused from the witness box. The defence was biding its time over the truth of her evidence.

The next prosecution witness was Mr Fenny, an old man who had worked in the same garret as John Fitter for ten months. He told the court that he had been in the workshop with him on Monday 10th April from about 2 o'clock until the murder had been discovered. He was not sure whether Fitter had gone downstairs at any time because he (Fenny) was very busy. Fitter could have left the room without him noticing.

When the prosecution produced a pair of pincers, the possible murder weapon, and asked Fenny whose they were, the old man was certain that they belonged to John Fitter. But when defence counsel produced a similar pair Fenny changed his story and said that he could not tell the difference. The old man was clearly an unsafe witness.

Their case bruised yet again, the prosecution summoned Sarah Divett's young playmate. The little lad told the court that he had seen Mr Fitter in the entry standing by his door and smoking a pipe at about 2.00 pm. He had been wearing his red soldier's jacket, but when the lad saw him again at about 3.00 pm the man was in shirt sleeves. Not wishing to give the boy any more unpleasant experiences the defence let him to leave the witness box without questioning.

The last witness for the prosecution was Mr Wood, the surgeon. He repeated all the evidence he had given at the inquest, but added that he had been shown a pair of pincers found by the authorities at Fitter's workplace. They had blood on them, but whose he could not say. When asked whether they were the murder weapon, he produced part of the Mrs Webb's skull. It had a hole in it about three quarters of an inch wide and large enough to be made by the pincers, but when asked by the defence if he were sure that the pincers were indeed the murder weapon he admitted that the hole "might also have been inflicted with a hammer or the head of a poker".

The prosecution's case finished, the defence began to dismantle the evidence. First they called Mrs Rufford, at whose house Mary Pattison had called. She agreed that Pattison had called at the time mentioned, but denied a conversation about boots. She insisted that that conversation happened days later and Mary Pattison must have confused the dates.

Mrs Dearns was called to corroborate that evidence. Mary Pattison, she said, had not taken the boots to Mr Fitter's until the Thursday after the murder, 13th April. She was certain of that because they were her boots and it was the first time in years that the box which contained them had been opened. Mrs Dearns told the court she thought it most unlikely that John Fitter would have stayed with blood on his hands in the cellar for long because she knew that he always kept a tub of water with soap down there, though she could not be certain that there was one there on the day of the murder.

Finally Mrs Dearns told the court that everyone knew John Fitter was poor and used the local pawnbroker. He often raised money from "trifling articles of female clothing" which he scrounged, but he was no murderer.

Mr Justice Taunton had heard enough. Summing up, he told the jury that every prosecution witness had been discredited in some way or other or their testimony proved flawed. It was still for the jury to decide their verdict, but he warned them that "it was much better that a guilty man should escape, even though guilty, than that an honest man should suffer". The jury agreed, and after only a few minutes they announced that John Fitter was "Not guilty".

Who then had killed Mrs Webb? In their speed to believe the witnesses and arrest John Fitter, had the police allowed the real culprit to escape? Or had they got the real murderer from the beginning but allowed him to go free because of poor investigations? No one ever found out.

Poached to Death
(Codsall 1887 - Express & Star)

Life must have seemed perfect to 28 year old Constable Brown on the evening of 6th August 1887. He was just setting out for a summer evening patrol of the countryside around Codsall near Wolverhampton, which was idyllic. To make matters even more perfect he had met and become engaged to the lovely Miss Bennet. They planned to marry in the near future.

His patrol would take him around the villages of Lane Green, Codsall and Pendeford where nothing much ever happened apart from the occasional drunk trying to find his way home along the twisting lanes. Knowing all the local people, Brown would often guide them on their way. In fact so friendly were the villagers that he very quickly knew everyone by their first names. This is why they were so horrified, when early on the morning of 7th August, the young man's corpse was found in the Shropshire Union Canal near Pendeford Bridge.

THE MYSTERIOUS DEATH OF A POLICEMAN NEAR CODSALL.

ADJOURNED INQUEST

Immediately rumours circulated that the young officer had been murdered. Nobody thought that an accident was possible because Constable Brown knew the area too well to fall into the canal. They were also certain that no villager could have killed him. It had to be some outsider, probably one of the many poachers who frequented the local pools and canal banks. When it was confirmed that he had died at around 4.00 am they were convinced.

But supposition has no place in criminal law and the purpose of the inquest at the Bull Inn, Codsall on 8th August was to find out whether Brown had died accidentally or been killed. For either verdict Mr Phillips, the coroner, was to rely heavily upon the expertise of Mr Fredrick Hawthorne, surgeon, and Dr Cooke of Tettenhall.

They reported that the constable's body showed no signs of external violence except for a slight swelling below the left ear. However, the brain was very congested with fluid blood as was the right auricle of the heart. The lungs themselves were congested, but not markedly so, and the stomach contained about half a pint of fluid.

It was that unusual lack of fluid which puzzled the coroner. Surely, he questioned, someone who had drowned would have swallowed a great deal of water in their vain attempt to escape? The two medical men agreed.

"Would the fact that he had not swallowed a large quantity of water," continued the coroner, " lead you to believe that he was insensible when he first entered the canal?" Once again they agreed. Mr Hawthorne added that the amount of fluid found in the stomach "was no more than one might expect to find of anyone who had died within some hours of a meal".

So if the young constable was not conscious when he entered the canal, how had he been rendered unconscious? The coroner turned to the evidence of the swelling on the officer's head and both surgeons agreed that it was only slight and had almost disappeared by the day of the post mortem, but undoubtedly Brown had been struck. They thought that his helmet had lessened the impact of the blow though it had still knocked him unconscious.

The Bull at Codsall where the inquest was held

"But did you discover any evidence that he had been struck?" enquired the coroner. At which point Inspector Cook produced the helmet and Mr Hawthorne pointed to where the blow had occurred. It must have been quite heavy because it had broken the cane rim of the helmet.

"If the officer had been rendered unconscious then he must have fallen to the ground?" continued the coroner. "Were there any signs to indicate that he had indeed been on the ground?"

"Oh yes," replied Mr Hawthorne. "He was covered in dust."
"Could he then have been dragged to the canal and thrown in?" continued the coroner. Both surgeons had to admit that they had found no evidence of drag marks on the uniform.

"So could he have been left unconscious near to the canal and when partially recovered staggered and fallen in himself?" asked Mr Phillips. Once again the surgeons pointed to the lack of fluid in the body.

"Even in a semi conscious state most people would sense water and try to escape," explained Mr Hawthorne.

However, there was further evidence to discount the idea that Brown was conscious. The examination had shown that his thumb was still trapped in his handcuffs as if he fallen onto them and caught his thumb. "If he had regained consciousness," continued Mr Hawthorne, "he would have undoubtedly have freed it while trying to escape the water."

The doctors' evidence complete, the coroner called the police to see whether they had found any evidence of a struggle near the canal. Unfortunately they had found nothing because that evening the towpath had been a busy with horses drawing boats and people from the local area and Wolverhampton. Mr Phillips turned to questioning the people who had come forward.

Thomas Hancox was an ironworker of Monmore Green, Wolverhampton who said that he had gone to fish in the canal at midnight with Emmanual Goucher, Isaiah Fletcher, William Whitmore and Benjamin Whitmore.

"We had moved to the two bridges above where the officer was pulled out and while we were there we must have seen about fifteen boatmen and anglers who passed us on their way to Stafford."
"And were any of them familiar to you?" asked the coroner.
"I only knew one of them who went by the nickname of Chub, sir," replied Hancox.

While they were there, he went on, Mr Tomkinson, the local gamekeeper, and Thomas Peak came up and tried to confiscate Goucher's rod, saying that they were all trespassing. Goucher had offered his name to the keeper rather than have his rod taken. During that confrontation the witness said that he had moved away from the canal bank and onto the bridge. The gamekeeper followed him but had allowed the men to fish further along the canal.

It was while fishing this new spot at about 4.30 am that they heard a body had been found by Pendeford Bridge. As they walked to the scene they met Thomas Peak again. He said that the corpse was the policeman and someone had found his helmet and stick close by. Tomkinson had gone to fetch the police. Hancox and friends stayed at the scene until the body was removed.

When Peak gave evidence he said that he had helped Tomkinson at nights from the previous May, but a week before the tragedy he had been asked by the gamekeeper to help in moving some young pheasants. He was to meet Tomkinson early on Sunday 7th August at Beach's Bridge.

"I arrived there at about 4 o'clock but Tomkinson was not there. I waited for over an hour and finally heard Tomkinson shouting 'Stop them!' He was chasing 15 to 20 men and finally caught up with one, Hancox, on a bridge which is about half a mile from Pendeford Bridge. I stayed with Hancox until Mr Tomkinson returned after chasing the others."

"It was while we were talking to Hancox that a young lad named Star came and said that a body had been found in the canal. We thought he was fooling around and told him to go away, but as we left the bridge we found a policeman's hat and broken cane. We also found an eel there," said Peak.
"An eel?" asked the startled coroner.
"Yes, sir, but Mr Tomkinson said to leave it for the police as it might be evidence. He then went off to find the police."

Eager to help, John Star told the court that he had left his home in North Street, Wolverhampton before 5 o'clock in the morning. He had joined the canal at Oxley and walked towards Pendeford Bridge.

"Not long after I arrived there two boats passed me and the first disturbed a body in the water. I turned to three anglers close by and pointed to the corpse. However, one of them was more interested in telling me that a poacher had stolen their fishing bag and had threatened them. As they did not seem particularly interested and did not want to help I told another angler and showed him the body. He also did not seem bothered. It was at that moment that I spotted the gamekeeper and told him, but he thought that I was fooling around and told me to clear off."

He waited until the body had been taken away then walked home. On his way he met another angler who lived in Warwick Street, Wolverhampton who told the young lad that his rod bag had been stolen that evening.

The coroner thanked the boy for his evidence then turned to questioning some anglers, but none of them could remember seeing Constable Brown that evening. The passing boatmen on the canal that night proved more difficult to trace, but one had come forward.

John Jenks of Brewood, a village north of Pendeford, worked the *Benaon* and on the morning of 7th August they had been on the Shropshire Union Canal. On board were his wife, a niece and some paying passengers - a Mr Challenor, his wife and son.

He had left Wolverhampton at 3.10 am in the company of the boat *Emily*.
"As we reached Pendeford Bridge, at about 6 o'clock a young man named Peter Turner, on a boat ahead of the *Emily*, shouted that there was a body in the water. Unfortunately it was too late for me to miss it and I bumped into it. There was a boy and a angler on the bank at the time."

There was nothing remarkable in Jenks's evidence about finding the body, but he went on to mention a curious incident which had happened earlier.

"At about half past 4 we had reached Autherley Junction when I saw a man carrying fishing tackle under his arm. He was going along the bank at tremendous speed as though he were being chased. He had a slight moustache and wore a cap and black jacket. He was heading towards Wolverhampton and seemed very flustered. I thought nothing more of it at the time, sir, but when the body was discovered I became worried."

"Would you recognise the man again?" asked the coroner.
"Yes, sir," came the instant reply. " I'd know him amongst a thousand."

Was Jenks's hurrying man the thief who had stolen the tackle of at least four anglers? Had he been stopped by PC Brown and killed him? The coroner had to dismiss the idea as pure conjecture, but told the jury that in his opinion the crime was that of murder. By a vote of 11 to1 they agreed and Mr Phillips adjourned the inquest wishing the police every success in their investigations. Hopefully, he added, there would be a speedy result because crimes against those whose job was to protect the public were most abhorrent.

Whether it was their fury at the death of a fellow officer or just enthusiasm, the police did act very swiftly. Having questioned people who lived close to the canal they discovered that a group of anglers had been fishing near

Pendeford Bridge on the fatal Saturday night. Better, they had a name, a certain William Ellis who was a bolt maker from George Street, Ettingshall. Unfortunately for Ellis he was already suspected by the police of poaching, so officers were immediately dispatched to his home.

In their haste to catch the murderer the police frightened Ellis with their intimidating approach and he refused to answer any questions. They decided to arrest him and on 9th August he was taken before the South Staffordshire Stipendary [magistrates] Court. There Detective Moreton told Mr Neville that they had arrested Ellis because he would not answer any questions about his movements at the weekend, except that he had gone fishing with four other men. Ellis's landlady confirmed that he had been away all weekend, arriving back late Sunday evening.

Mr Neville asked Ellis to make a statement. Ellis replied,
"I did go fishing on the Saturday night. I met four other men and we went to the public house and remained there until 10 o'clock. We then started fishing again. I caught several fish, but did not see anything of the policeman."

When asked why he would not tell the police the names of his associates, Ellis said,
"I thought they were trying to do us for poaching and so I wouldn't tell on my mates."

Having realised the seriousness of the situation Ellis then gave the names of the four men to the court, but he was remanded in custody until his story could be verified. By the time of the next hearing on 12th August Ellis's friends had been traced and his story proved true. Mr Neville, probably annoyed with Ellis for wasting the time of the police and the court, discharged him, but severely warned him of his behaviour. Perhaps to frighten him, the magistrate bound him over to appear at a future hearing, though it never happened.

When Ellis had left, though, the magistrate had strong words for the police about their over zealous conduct. He warned them to be more cautious in future before arresting innocent people and wasting court time.

By the time that the adjourned inquest opened on 30th August at the Bull Inn, Codsall, the police had certainly been more thorough. They had interviewed everyone in the surrounding area and built up an almost complete picture of Constable Brown's movements before midnight on the fatal evening. Unfortunately they had found no one who could confirm where he might have been after midnight.

Mr Phillips, the coroner, knew what had happened at the magistrates court and did not want a fiasco of his own. He warned the police and witnesses that he would listen to no rumour or supposition. Facts were all that concerned his court. Mindful of their mistake, the police produced witnesses who could clearly establish Constable Brown's movements on 6th August.

First to appear was Henry Lees, an iron plate worker from Steward Street, Wolverhampton. He testified that he had gone to the Woodman Inn in Lane Green at about 8.30 pm that evening with friends. At about 9 o'clock the young officer had entered but had not spoken to anyone, nor did he have anything to drink. He had simply looked all around the bar, then left.

Questioned by the coroner, Lees said that he was not certain if the constable was looking for anyone in particular, but he did seem in a hurry. Lees's friends, who were not at the inquest, had agreed with the statement.

William Meddlicott, a labourer from Bilbrook, told the hearing that he had seen the constable at 8 o'clock on the Saturday evening heading towards Lane Green. He himself had walked to Lane Green with a friend, James Craik, and had arrived at the Woodman Inn around 9.30. They had left there just before closing time and gone to Craik's house, but they had not seen the officer again. They were told that Brown had been in the inn looking around, though they had not actually seen him.

The next witness was Mrs Susan Bird who lived in Lane Green. She had seen the constable close to her house at about half past 9. He was alone and seemed to be heading in the direction of the Greyhound Inn. That was precisely where he was going, because the landlady, Mrs Anne Parker, said that he had been in her pub shortly after 9.30. Once again he had looked all round the taproom where seven or eight men were drinking. They had asked him to join them, but he had refused. As he was leaving he had asked the landlady if she had seen William Meddlicott that evening as his brother, Thomas Meddlicott, was in The Woodman. She had replied that she had not.

Mr Phillips asked why Constable Brown would be asking after Meddlicott and Anne Parker replied, "He knew the brothers well and thought that they might like to drink together." When asked about the constable's demeanour that evening she said that he had seemed in rather a hurry.

Calling at two pubs with the same unusual behaviour? Was Brown searching for someone in particular? Had he been tipped off about some possible crime and was trying to find the villain? Whatever the cause, the villagers knew that that something was wrong that evening.

Brown's strange behaviour was also mentioned by the next witnesses. Mrs Sarah Jane Grosvenor had been at her bedroom window just after the pubs had shut at around 10.30 pm. She had noticed Brown alone in the village square and he seemed to be watching the pub to see when the lights would be turned out. He was standing leaning on his stick. She remembered the time, just after 11.00 pm, because she had remarked on his unusual behaviour to her husband when she got into bed.

It would seem that Mrs Grosvenor was the last person to see PC Brown alive, except for his murderer or murderers. No more was seen or heard of him until his corpse was found in the canal. Whoever Brown came across later must have dispatched him quickly and quietly because no one in the area heard anything suspicious.

George Sneade was a waggoner who lived in Pendeford. He told the court that he had been carrying hay in a field by Pendeford Bridge until 9.30 on the Saturday night. He had turned his horses out into the field over the bridge at about 11 o'clock and walked back home which was some 100 yards from the bridge. He had seen no one about at the time, nor did he hear any disturbance during the night. He had retired to bed well after midnight and only knew of the body at 9 o'clock the following morning.

George Wrighton, groom and coachman to Mr Martin of The Birches, Codsall, said that he lived in a cottage in the grounds of The Birches and not too far from Pendeford Bridge. That Saturday evening he had sat on his garden wall relaxing before going to bed. It was about 11.30 when he thought he heard a man holloaing across the fields in the direction of Pendeford. He told the court that the cry was like one person shouting softly to another. But it died down and after everything had gone quiet he went to bed.

If Wrighton was correct and he had heard cries of distress then no one else had heard them, especially one Richard Hammond. Hammond was a boatman working for the Shropshire Union Canal Company and that evening before midnight he had moored his boat, *The Courier*, close to Pendeford Bridge. There he had remained until after 4.00 am when he resumed his journey. He testified that he had heard nothing untoward during that evening.

Hammond of all people would have been expected to hear any sort of commotion, especially if someone was fighting for their life, but he heard nothing. In fact the coroner asked him if he were sure to which Hammond replied, "I was amazed to learn that a body had been found so close to where I moored my boat, sir."

As further witnesses gave their evidence Constable Brown's murder became all the more mysterious. Try as the court might there seemed to be no definite motive. Perhaps the most likely was that which the villagers had rumoured all along - that the young policeman had been killed when he intercepted poachers.

It was that line of inquiry which had led the police to check on possible stories of poachers, and there was one which might just explain PC Brown's death.

Thomas White of Paradise Street, Wolverhampton had reported to the gamekeeper, Tomkinson, that he and a friend named Kettle had seen two suspicious characters walking about the estate on the August Bank Holiday (then the first weekend in August). As a reward for their honesty Tomkinson had told them to meet him at the Wheel Inn on the following Saturday and he would give them some fish.

As arranged they met at the Wheel Inn on 6th August and later went to The Woodman. From there all three went to the gamekeeper's house, having purchased a gallon of beer and something to eat. After a chat and a smoke they slept until 4 o'clock when they all went to the canal. There they met a number of anglers whom Tomkinson chased away, amongst whom were Goucher and Hancox. When White and Kettle had got their fish they left the gamekeeper who headed back towards the canal.

White's evidence corroborated that given by the anglers at the initial inquest and, incidentally, also cleared Tomkinson of any implication in the affair. It was not unknown for gamekeepers to poach their master's stock. To make certain of the gamekeeper the police had interviewed Mrs Tomkinson and her two sons. They all confirmed the events of the Saturday evening.

At the close of the inquest the court was no nearer to finding out why PC Brown had been so brutally murdered or who the assassins might have been. Despite further lengthy investigations, that is how it remains today.

There was a sad little postscript which summed up the tragedy. On 9th August the young policeman was buried at Codsall church, Miss Bennet burying her husband to be. She "was very much distressed at the graveside and quite broke down". The Reverend Tooth tried desperately to comfort her, but must have realised that part of her had been murdered too.

Innocent as the Angels
(Bradley 1857 - The Chronicle)

Elizabeth Hopley was the daughter of a farmer at Wem in Shropshire. There was little work in the area, so at age of 18 she left the farm and moved in with her aunt and uncle, Mr and Mrs Wetton, at Bradley near Wolverhampton.

Here she found a job with Philip Clare, owner of a local "butty mine". These were nothing to do with Ken Dodd, but small pits bought by small local businessmen to dig out the remains of the coal from larger collieries. They sold it at a contracted price. Elizabeth was a "banks worker" looking after the equipment above ground.

In all these pits the supply of coal was limited, and in March 1857 Clare dismissed Elizabeth because his mine was running down. She was not downhearted. She had a boyfriend, Martin Egan, and her aunt and uncle were only too happy for her to stay with them while she found other work. Quite soon she got a job with Mr Moon who owned a local factory, but happiness for Elizabeth was not to last.

On the morning of 30th April 1857 George Buckley, a labourer, and his son were on their way to work at Lea Brook. Walking along the Bradley Arm of the Birmingham Canal near Mr David Rose's Wharf they came across a body floating on its belly in about 5 feet of water. As the bank was newly made up Buckley needed help to reach the corpse so his son fetched the police. The body was taken to the Swan Inn where it was examined. Elizabeth Hopley was dead, but by what means?

> **THE ALLEDGED MURDER AT BRADLEY.**
> PHILIP CLARE, 30, miner, was indicted for the wilful murder of Elizabeth Hopley at Bradley near Bilston, on the 29th of April, 1857. He seemed but little disconcerted by the serious position in which he was placed, and pleaded "not guilty" in a firm clear voice.

The task of telling the girl's family was left to the police, and at the Wetton's home they enquired about Elizabeth's frame of mind on the previous evening. Aunt Jane Wetton told them that her niece had been happy when she left the house at 10 o'clock to see her young man. She had a message for him and said that she would not be gone long, which is why she did not take her bonnet or shawl.

The police asked why they had not been worried when Elizabeth didn't return. Jane said she thought her niece had stayed with neighbours, but the police were suspicious and questioned her about her relationship the girl.

"We were quite good friends," Mrs Wetton replied, "and never quarrelled." Occasionally she had spoken to the girl as most adults did with young people, but there had been no serious clash. On the night before Elizabeth left the house Jane had told her off for not filling Mr Davis's bath. He was their lodger. Their conversation was not a quarrel, more like a disagreement.

Asked whether Elizabeth had any quarrels with other people, Mrs Wetton said that as far as she knew there was no "cause of anger or ill-feeling against anyone".

There had been a dispute though, with Philip Clare, Elizabeth's employer, whom Elizabeth had taken to Bilston Magistrates Court on 3rd March 1857. He had paid her in "Tommy notes" which proved worthless and the court had forced Clare to pay Elizabeth in real money.

[Tommy notes, coins and tokens were commonly issued by employers instead of money. They forced people to buy highly priced, low quality goods from local stores which were often owned by the employer. The practice was made a criminal offence by the Truck Acts of 1831/7.]

When news of the tragedy spread people remembered the disagreement between Philip Clare and the young girl and rumours soon linked her death to him. To make matters worse for himself, he spread gossip about Elizabeth, telling people that he had advanced her money because she had a venereal disease and needed to see a doctor urgently. But the rumours concerning Clare and his young employee continued to spread and Clare announced that he would be at the inquest to finish the gossip once and for all. It only made things worse when he did not turn up and told neighbours that if the police wanted him, they must fetch him.

But the police could not act because they had no concrete evidence which might link Clare to Elizabeth's death, and by mid May they were lost for a lead. Then on 23rd May they had their first breakthrough.

George Powell arrived at Bradley Police Station looking terrified. Highly emotional, he could barely tell his story for fear of being overheard. No longer able to conceal his dreadful secret, he had told his landlady and the other lodger the night before and they had forced him to reveal everything to the police.

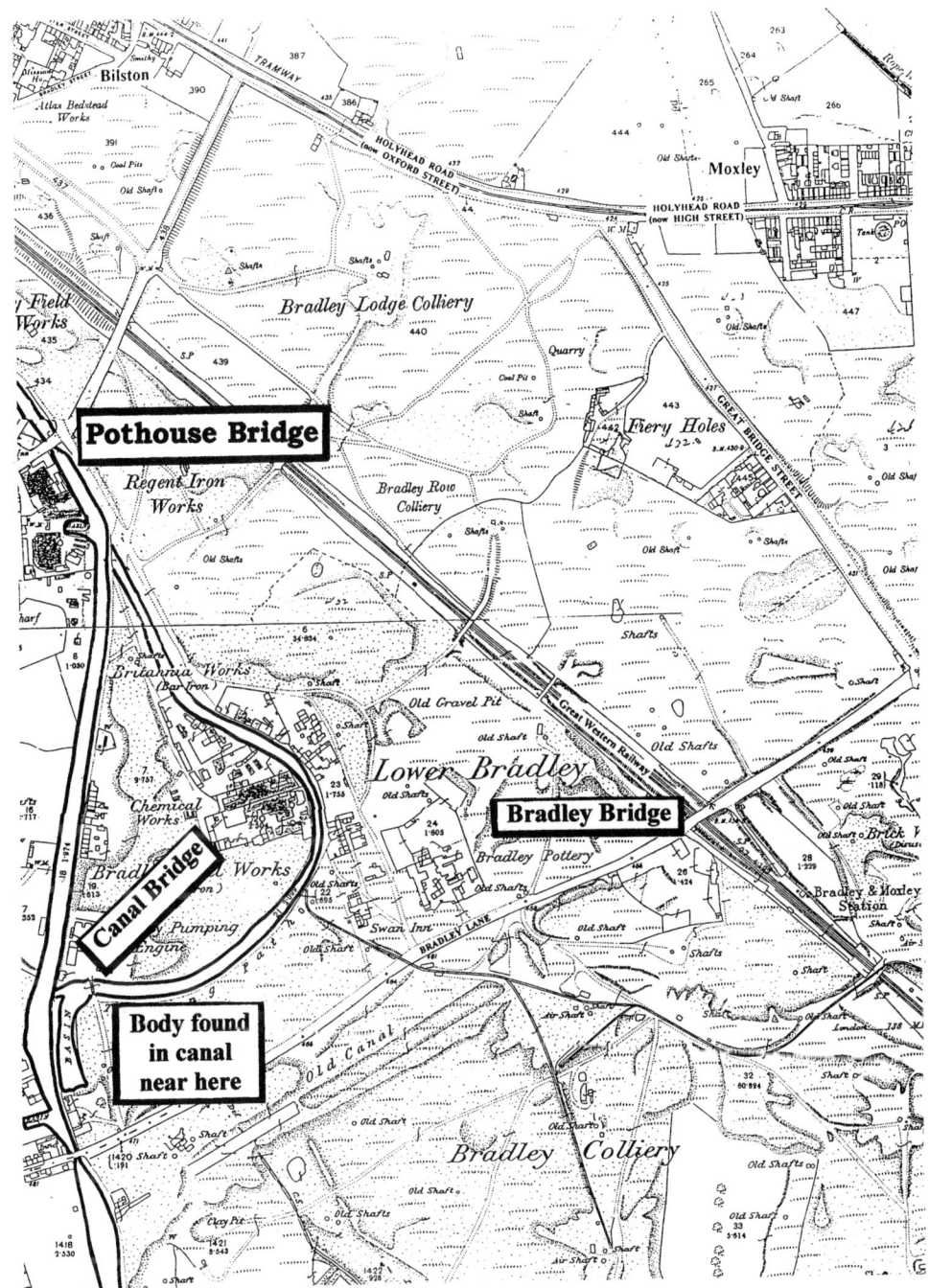

On this part of the 1887 OS map Bilston is top left and Moxley top right. The canal is the Wednesbury Oak Loop which ran from the Birmingham Main line to the Walsall Canal. About half of it has been filled in and it now runs no further than Bradley Lane, bottom.

He was the night watchman at Mr David Rose's Colliery Wharf which was next to Philip Clare's pit. He knew Clare well because Clare had asked him to keep an eye on the pit at night. On the evening of 29th April he had set off on his rounds at midnight. He knew the exact time because he had heard the Moxley clock strike twelve just as he started. As he had a crippled leg he moved slowly, and he always kept to the shadows for fear of trespassers.

As he neared the canal bridge he saw two people on it arguing. From the shadows he heard a woman exclaim, "Don't kill me, Philip." But the man struck her with his fist and she fell. Feeling terrified, but not knowing what was going to happen, he approached the man, who was Philip Clare. By the time he got close Clare had the girl in his arms, and not noticing the watchman, he threw the body into the canal. The girl must have been unconscious because she did not struggle or scream when she hit the water.

Turning round, Clare saw George Powell and threatened to kill him too if he dared utter a word to anyone. He continued those threats as they walked back to the shed which the watchman used as a shelter.

When the police asked why he had taken so long to report the story, Powell confessed that he was terrified of what might happen to him. Clare kept meeting him and issuing the same threat. On one occasion Clare sent another man to warn him. Later Clare waylaid him between Bilston Gate and the Blue Boar and said, 'If you talk about that job I will kill you. I'll serve you the same way as I served her. I will set someone else on to watch you.' That was at 11 o'clock on 11th May.

The police reported that whilst giving his evidence Powell frequently cried like a baby, and so sure were they of his statement that they went immediately to search for Clare. Later that day he was arrested to await the next magistrate's hearing.

At the hearing on 20th May 1857 Clare looked so pale that the magistrate, John Leigh Esq, commented that he must be guilty if he looked so terrible. So much for deciding guilt or innocence on valid evidence. Clare replied that he was distressed due to the loss of a horse. He could not afford to replace it and therefore his business might fail. His paleness had nothing to do with his being accused of murder, which he had not done. But Mr Leigh was not put off and remanded him in police custody until more evidence was available.

When the case resumed at the beginning of June the police had found several witnesses who could give evidence as to Philip Clare's whereabouts on the night of 29th April.

George Haines, the local police officer, reported that he had spoken to Clare at about 12 o'clock on that evening. He had been on duty on the turnpike road called the Great Holyhead Road when he saw Clare going towards his home. He was about 70 yards from his house when the officer spoke to him.

That placed Clare in the area of the canal at the time of the crime, but the next witness's evidence was to be more damning. Elizabeth Ellmore told the court that she lived in Moxley opposite Clare's house. She had been up late that night as one of her family was ill, and at about 1 o'clock she had seen him coming up the road towards his home. She remembered that he had come from the direction of the bridge and seemed the worse for drink. She also testified that he had walked straight past John Plant's house and had not entered it. However, under questioning she had to admit that she did not possess a clock.

But John Plant, the next witness, refuted what Mrs Ellmore had said. Clare had indeed visited him at about midnight on the 29th April and the two of them had chatted for about two hours before Clare left. As both of them were "butty owners" they had talked about the future of their respective pits. Plant insisted that Clare had not left until at least 2 o'clock and had gone straight home.

With that disagreement on Clare's whereabouts the police would rely heavily on Powell's evidence if they were to have Philip Clare sent for trial. But Powell had vanished. He had last been seen boarding a train for Dudley and had not reappeared. The magistrates had no option but to abandon the hearing and allow Clare to go free.

By the date of the next hearing on 27th June Powell had still not been traced despite warrants being issued throughout the area. By late August though, the police had a stroke of luck. Powell had surfaced in Warwick where he had been committed to goal for breaking the windows at a workhouse when the guardians refused him relief.

On 30th August the final magistrates' court hearing took place and Powell repeated his damning evidence. The bench were satisfied that Clare had a case to answer and remanded him to await trial at Stafford Assizes. Before Clare left the court he was allowed to make a statement. He flatly denied having anything to do with the death of Elizabeth Hopley adding, "I am no murderer. I'm as innocent as the angels on their thrones in Heaven. I'm as innocent as God who sits upon his own throne." It would be for the Assize Court to see if that was so.

Clare's trial began in Stafford on 16th December 1857. Deeply divided, the people of Bradley packed the court and the surrounding area, and from the outset it seemed as though their uncertainties would be repeated in the courtroom. Such was the evidence that it became difficult for the judge and jury to decide even whether a crime had been committed.

*Pothouse Bridge
(see top of map)
with explanatory plaque.*

The first witness was Mr Henry Dewes Best, the surgeon who had examined Elizabeth Hopley's corpse. On 2nd May he had performed the post mortem and found a slight discoloration on the shoulders and at the back of the neck. He had also discovered two recent scratches on the right hand, which might have been caused by the body coming into contact with a rough surface, like a wall or the ground. In his opinion they might have been caused by the victim herself. The body itself was very rigid and the hands firmly clenched.

In Mr Best's opinion the girl had died from asphyxia or suffocation from immersion in the water. Controversially, he thought she had been conscious when she entered the water and quite able to move her limbs. Also, as she was a healthy and remarkably muscular young woman he thought that "she would be able to make considerable resistance to one person".

Questioned by Mr Kettle for the defence, the surgeon reaffirmed his view that she was not "in a state of insensibility when she got into the water". As to the marks on her neck and back, in his opinion "the discoloration was not caused by violence". But possibly most damning for the prosecution was Mr Best's view that "if she had been partially sensible when put into the water then he would not have expected to find any evidence of struggling on the body. The abrasions on the body and the position of the limbs indicated great struggling in the water". Later he confirmed that he had found no evidence that Elizabeth Hopley had been struggling with a man, meaning that her only injuries were abrasions caused by her thrashing hands striking the bank or bottom.

Asked by Mr Kettle to suggest a possible cause of death, Mr Best offered a non medical opinion.

"I am in the habit of going into the colliery district at night. A coke hearth is a very dazzling object. Large fires on the ground give an uncertain, flickering light and throw lateral shadows. The bank was a foot and a half or two feet above the surface of the water. ... I think that coming to the angle where the two branches of the canal diverge, she fell off the bank into the water."

This is conjecture, but interesting in view of later evidence.

Despite his detailed questioning, Mr Scotland for the prosecution could not get the surgeon to vary his opinion, so he tried to place Clare at the scene at the time of Elizabeth's death. Presumed scene and presumed time. There was no reliable evidence to fix either, but for some reason the barristers and the judge seem to have accepted the time according to George Powell who had not yet been heard in this court.

Previous witnesses at the magistrates' court gave their evidence again, with Elizabeth Ellmore insisting that she had seen Clare at 1 o'clock and John Plant saying that Clare had been with him from midnight until 2 am.

PC Haines also stood by his previous evidence. He was certain that he had met Clare at midnight on the Hollyhead Road. Clare was 300 or 400 yards nearer to his own home in Moxley than he was to the turn off to Fiery Holes, being only 70 yards from his own house.

Fiery Holes was a small group of pit houses between Moxley and the Great Western Railway. Tracks from there lead to the railway bridge and then to the canal. Having visited the scene I reckoned that the walk would take ten or fifteen minutes, making it at least 12.10 before Clare could reach the canal.

John Clewley worked in the iron rolling trade and lived at Moxley. On the night of 29th April he was on the road between Moxley and Bilston when he saw Philip Clare below Pothouse Bridge on the Sedgeley Road, which was about half a mile from his house. It was between 6 and 7 o'clock and Clare was talking to one George Griffiths. He did not see him again.

Edward Lloyd was landlord of the Square & Compasses in Oxford Street, Bilston.. He said that Clare was in his pub at half past 6. A man named Wooliscroft came in and sat with Clare until they left at about 11 o'clock. Clare lived about a mile from the pub.

Edward Wooliscroft confirmed the landlord's statement, adding that he and Clare left the pub together and walked towards Moxley for about 400 yards. He then turned to go into his own house in Temple Street and Clare continued on his way towards Moxley. By the time the witness reached home it was 11.30. Clare "would have had to pass by the road to Fiery Holes on his way home."

Despite the succession of witnesses the prosecution could not actually place Clare at the bridge at the presumed time of Elizabeth Hopley's death, but the next witness did have some alarming evidence.

Samuel Hawes was a watchman for the Great Western Railway. On the night of 29th April he was on duty with another watchman, named Watson, and their duty was to keep watch on the Bradley Bridge. At about 9.45 Watson left his post to make a drink for the two men. It seems that they were in the habit of sitting in a small hovel close by for a drink to get out of the cold.

After Watson had left at about 11 o'clock, Hawes told the court, he heard a man and a woman speaking on the railway bridge. The conversation could not have been that interesting because Hawes left his post and went to the hovel. He had to admit that he had fallen asleep.

He was suddenly awoken by a loud screaming and heard the woman exclaim, "Don't hit me!" "I left the hovel to investigate, but could see no one. I could hear voices. As nothing else seemed to be happening I returned to the hovel and sat down for about twenty minutes. Then I went up the line and saw the goods train coming. It was due in Bilston at 11.40 pm. When I later checked its time of arrival at the station it was recorded at 11.45 pm on that night."

During questioning Hawes had to admit that at no time had he actually seen anyone on the bridge, he had just heard voices and the man's voice had not talked of violence. Crucially the prosecution still could not place Philip Clare near the scene of the crime, but they still had their trump card, George Powell, and he was the next witness.

Powell was as adamant as he had been to the police that he had seen both Philip Clare and Elizabeth Hopley on the canal bridge that night. He was certain that Clare had struck the girl and thrown her unconscious corpse into the canal. Once again he repeated that he had been threatened so much that he had had to escape the area. Mr Scotland for the prosecution was elated. At last he could prove Clare's involvement in the murder, or so he thought.

When the defence counsel, Mr Kettle, began to cross examine Powell matters took a different turn. Immediately Powell had to admit that his real name was Samuel Wall. "I have passed in the name of George Powell," the witness said meekly, "and also may have passed in other names but I have forgotten them."

Wall had changed his name of his own accord when his father died in 1843. He had lived with his father but after suffering a leg injury in 1840 he had moved around the area selling memorandum books and religious tracts. Though obviously not a crime, this information did produce the first doubts of the witness's reliability. More was to follow.

"And could you tell the court of another crime you witnessed on the same canal some years earlier?" Mr Kettle demanded.

Wall looked visibly shocked, but according to *The Chronicle's* court reporter managed to mumble, "This is the first time that I have seen anything of this kind on the canal. I do not recollect giving information to Sub Inspector Costello about something I had seen happen on the bank of the canal on a former occasion. I did not tell a person named Smith anything of the kind. I heard of a child being found in the canal, but I never heard that I was wanted to attend the inquest."

Mr Kettle continued. "Why did you disappear from the area for such a long time?"
"I went away because I was afraid for my life," blurted Wall.
"And where did you go and why did you return?" continued Kettle.

Wall told the court that he had been sacked from his job as watchman because his employer found out that he had left his post to go to the police. When he left Bradley Wall had travelled from Dudley to Worcester and then on to Bristol, where he stayed in a workhouse for about a week. He then travelled to Bath and finally came to Warwick where he had been arrested for breaking the guardian's window. When the police brought him back to the area they placed him in a workhouse in Sedgeley for his safety.

"Safe from what?" Kettle asked.
"From Clare and his brother, George," pleaded Wall.
"And who forced you to go to the police?" asked Mr Kettle.
"The woman I was lodging with at New Town, Bilston," said Wall.

Mr Kettle put it to Wall that the only reason that he ran away from the area and had taken so long to come forward in the first place was because the whole story was a lie. Wall was terrified of being found out as he had been in the previous incident. Wall flatly denied it but the doubts mounted. However, realising that the man would not change his story because if he did he risked goal for perjury, Mr Kettle dismissed him.

The final witness added further doubt to the whole case. Was any crime committed at all? Superintendent Hugh M'Crea of Bilston Police Station told the court that he had taken Philip Clare into custody on 24th May. When charged with drowning the girl Clare had protested his innocence. Knowing the prisoner quite well, the officer had an inclination to believe him, but still made detailed investigations at the crime scene.

Having questioned many local people he became suspicious of the area. "It would seem, my lord, that frequently accidents have happened in that area to people walking in the open coalfields at night. The lights from the coke fires, always alight in that vicinity, can make it very difficult for people to see where they are going. In fact, since these assizes began a man has fallen into the canal and has drowned about half a mile from where Elizabeth Hopley's body was found."

The courtroom buzzed with excitement. The judge, obviously concerned by the Superintendent's evidence, brought the trial to a rapid end. In his summing up he emphasised all the main arguments, but had to tell the jury that he had never before heard such "a perfect alibi presented to a jury".

He must have been referring to Powell's evidence of the time when the crime was committed, because there was no other evidence on the point, and the fact that Clare had witnesses to "prove" that he was elsewhere. "Even prosecution witnesses had testified to that fact," said the judge.

The jury had no hesitation in declaring the prisoner not guilty and Philip Clare was discharged.

With witnesses vague or unreliable or both, and with Superintendent M'Crae's evidence throwing doubt on the root of the murder charge, the verdict is unquestionably correct. But the case leaves many questions.

What of Elizabeth Hopley's boyfriend, Martin Egan? Aunt Jane Wetton had told the police that she left the house to meet him at 10.00 pm. Egan did give evidence at the trial, which I did not report because all he said was that they had met at 6.00 pm and not again. Egan was not cross examined, just believed. So at 10.00 pm was Elizabeth really going to meet Martin or someone else? What was she doing near the canal? Had she been murdered or was she the victim of a tragic accident?

Had Powell/Wall's landlady and co-lodger anything to say about having 'forced' him to go to the police?

How could the judge come to such an extraordinary conclusion about Clare's alibi. The only evidence as to the time was that of Powell/Shaw, which was, to say the least, unreliable? There being no reliable or clear evidence about the time of the girl's death, why did everyone seem to assume that she went into the water around midnight? It might have been hours earlier or later.

And what of Powell/Wall? Why had he insisted that he had seen a murder take place? Psychologists today would have a field day trying to work him out. He seems to have carried no grudge against Clare because the lives of the two had never crossed. Was it the pathetic attempt of a person so crippled by life and so depressed that he looked for some fame by making up wild stories? Or had he actually seen something dreadful that evening?

Note that Powell/Wall's evidence and that of Samuel Hawes both feature a man and a woman on a bridge and the woman pleading with the man not to harm her. One bridge is over a canal and the other a railway, so one man's evidence must be irrelevant, or are we all going mad?

The police made further investigations but nothing ever came of them. As one reporter in the *Staffordshire Advertiser* wrote on 19th December, "One prevailing feature of the case is a mystery so dark that little hope can be entertained that it will ever be solved." It never was.

Stabbing in Fleet Street
(Birmingham 1879 – B'ham Daily Gazette)

People have always looked for ways to put off paying for things, from Provident Checks, to hire purchase, to credit cards. The difference between the 19th and the 21st centuries is that now we rarely see the faces of our creditors or the people who collect the money for them. Not so long ago the tallyman would call, we called him the "never-never man", to ask for his weekly or monthly payment. He made sure that he called on Friday evening or early Saturday morning and was always ready for the excuse and the bad tempered debtor.

Thomas Russell was a 61 year old warehouseman who lived in Tennant Street, Birmingham. He made his living by selling clothing and other household goods from his warehouse to those who could rarely afford cash. That was the easy part of his job, the difficult bit was trying to collect the payments. As he was only a small businessman he had to do it himself and he never enjoyed the prospect. As he often told his friends, "You never know what reaction you are likely to get when you knock their door, they might even try to hit you."

At about 11.30 pm on Saturday 28th June 1879 Thomas Russell was walking up Fleet Street, which still runs between Summer Hill and Newhall Street. It was then a notoriously rough part of Birmingham. Not knowing the street, he was examining the houses carefully to make sure that he knocked on the right door when he was stopped by a Mrs Cawley who wanted to know what he was doing.

Before he had time to say anything a small crowd gathered around him. Feeling menaced, he tried to escape, but the cat calling crowd followed him down the street.

Suddenly one of the women screamed out that she had been stabbed and fell to the ground. In the ensuing panic Russell managed to free himself and dash away, but he was horrified to hear that the crowd were accusing him of the crime and that he was being chased by some men. They overtook him near the corner of Great Charles Street and Congreve Street where they held him until a police officer arrived.

Partly to pacify the crowd and partly for Russell's own safety, Constable Pittaway decided to take him into custody, but even as they walked to the station Russell was harried by the crowd. Before Pittaway left the incident he had also made sure that the injured woman was taken to the General Hospital.

Here the injured Caroline Brookes was looked after by Mr Hawkins who discovered a stab wound under her right arm. Having made sure that the weapon had not pierced the chest wall, he dressed the wound and sent the woman home, telling her to return the following morning, Monday 30th. She did so and there were no serious symptoms so she was allowed home again. When she came back the next day though, pleurisy was detected and Caroline Brookes was admitted under the care of Mr Jolly. By the next day she had caught pneumonia of the right lung and gradually deteriorated until she died at about 2 o'clock on Thursday 10th July.

Thomas Russell had been in custody on charges of assault but now the police were not short of witnesses who would say that he killed Caroline Brookes and he was charged with murder. On 11th July 1879 Russell appeared at the Birmingham Public Office before magistrates Hill, Wright, Lloyd and Ratcliffe.

First to give evidence was Ann Cawley who lived at 13 Fleet Street. She told the court that at about 11.30 on the evening of 28th June she saw Thomas Russell examining the door of her house. When she challenged him he walked away, but she followed and asked him what he was doing. He turned round and without warning threatened her. He said, "You will know on Monday night to your sorrow. Now go away from me or I will chivey you, for I mean to chivey someone before I leave the street tonight."

"Chivey?" queried the one magistrate.
"Beat or hit someone, sir," replied Mrs Cawley, and then continued.

Russell, she said, had passed Caroline Brookes and a man called Bruton, who were standing at the top of an entry. All three followed the prisoner down the street, but not together, when he suddenly turned round and struck Caroline Brookes under the right arm. He ran away then and Bruton chased after him.

Meanwhile Ann Cawley went to Brookes and found her on the floor with blood coming from her arm. When the police officer came the injured girl was put into a cab and taken to the hospital.

William Bruton also lived in Fleet Street. He and Caroline Brookes had eaten supper in his house and then walked out afterwards around the streets. When they reached the top of one entry in Fleet Street they saw Thomas Russell followed by Mrs Cawley. They decided to follow him, but after about 14 yards the man turned round and struck Caroline under the arm, then ran away.

"I believe the prisoner had a knife, sir, as I saw something flash in the light from the street lamp. Caroline fell at my feet and cried out, 'Oh, Bill, the knife! I have been stabbed.' I chased after him and was never more than 5 yards behind and never lost sight of him until he was arrested in Congreve Street."

He told the court that as he ran he shouted, "Stop him!" and because of that was joined in the chase by Thomas Hubble and others.

Hubble of 15 Lionel Street confirmed what Bruton had said and added that he had seen everything, including the attack with the knife. He said that when both he and Bruton reached Russell he was surrounded by a crowd.

Mary Owen of Fleet Street told the court that she had been standing at her entry in the street when she noticed a tall man pass by. He was being followed by a group of people when he turned round and struck Brookes under the arm. Bruton had chased the man shouting 'Murder!'

Strangely, when questioned she denied that any stones were thrown at Russell or that there was a crowd in the street. Only when Russell was being chased did other men appear. Equally strange, the magistrates did not take up the point about possible harassment of the prisoner, but it was to surface again.

Edward Heath was a groom from Fleet Street who said that he was at home on the evening of 28th June when he heard shouts of 'Murder!' He went into the street and saw Russell and Bruton running towards him. He managed to catch Russell and handed him over to two young men while he went indoors to put on his boots. When he came out again Russell had broken free and run off up Summer Row. Heath followed and caught him in Congreve Street.

The final prosecution witness was Constable Pittaway. He was on duty in Newhall Street when a woman came running up to him to say there had been a row in Fleet Street where a woman had been stabbed. He went there and found the victim lying on the footpath with blood coming from a wound in her right side. He told the people present to take her to the hospital and at that point he was told that the attacker had run up Summer Row. He followed and met a crowd of people standing round the prisoner in Congreve Street. He arrested the prisoner and took him to the police station.

"Did the prisoner have anything to say?" asked one magistrate.
"He said that he hadn't stabbed anyone, your honour," replied the constable.
"What was his behaviour like at that time?" asked the magistrate.

Pittaway said that Russell became violent and threw himself on the ground protesting his innocence. At that point the crowd began to hit him so the constable rescued the man and took him the police station. During their walk Russell told Pittaway that he had been stoned by the people from Fleet Street and that was why he had run away. He also said, 'If this is proved against me I am a ruined man.' Once at the police station he was searched but no knife was found. When charged with the incident he said, 'I have stabbed no one.'

Constable Pittaway added that Russell was obviously frightened but could not say whether that was because he was innocent or terrified because of his guilt. Undoubtedly the occupants of Fleet Street had frightened him, but how violent they had been and when that violence began the police had not yet clarified.

However, one witness came forward who helped Russell's case. Mary Johnson of Fleet Street told the magistrates that when Mrs Cawley discovered Russell at her door she grabbed hold of him and shook him. During that confrontation a group of boys appeared and began to call after the prisoner, but she did not see him stoned or hit, nor had she seen the stabbing of Caroline Brookes.

It was obvious to the court that some sort of commotion had taken place in Fleet Street on the evening of 28th June and because of it Caroline Brookes had died. With so many witnesses saying that Russell had struck the fatal blow, the magistrates had no option but to remand him on a charge of murder and commit him for trial at Warwick Assizes. Meanwhile the police set about trying to find out exactly what had happened in Fleet Street that evening.

By the time of the Assize hearing on 7th August 1879 the police had gathered a good number of people who could give evidence on Thomas Russell's behalf. Most were character witnesses, but there were others from Fleet Street itself. However, before the trial really began Mr Justice Thesiger almost stopped it.

The prosecution, represented by Mr Soden and Mr Dawson, wanted to produce the dying woman's deposition [written statement] as evidence. This was important to their case because the Victorian courts treated dying declarations as invariably truthful. They were always reported by someone else and therefore hearsay, so the law of evidence imposed several conditions on them. When asked by the judge if Thomas Russell had been told the importance of the deposition in any possible trial, the prosecution had to admit that he had not.

[For another case involving a dying declaration see 'The Voice of the Dead' in Tony Hunt's previous book *Accident, Manslaughter or Murder*, QuercuS 2001.]

"He had," said Mr Soden, "been taken before the magistrates and was told that the girl was in a dangerous condition and that he would be taken to the hospital so that her statement could be taken, but nothing was said further about any charge".

Mr Leigh, the defence counsel, intervened, telling the judge that his client had not been represented at the hospital by a solicitor nor had he been told of his right to ask questions of the girl. "The prisoner was not told in legal form what the charge against him was," continued Mr Leigh.

The judge became very annoyed with the prosecution.

"How could the prisoner be examined and cross examined unless he knew the specific nature of the charges?" And turning to Mr Leigh he said, "Your objection to the deposition of the deceased is that the prisoner did not know the exact nature of the charges."

"Yes, my lord," declared Mr Leigh. "Under those circumstances the deposition is not admissible."

Mr Justice Thesiger was clearly disturbed by this lack of professionalism, but wanting the trial to continue he retired to consult another judge. After advice from Mr Justice Lindley, he allowed the case to continue and the deposition to be used in evidence, but warned the prosecution that the jury would take into consideration the failure in procedure if necessary.

The prosecution had found no further witnesses and so each of them in turn repeated what they had said in the magistrates' court. The defence cross examination was intended to show that these witnesses were untrustworthy and prone to violence, especially towards strangers.

Ann Cawley denied attacking the prisoner by grabbing hold of him. She said that she had backed away as he seemed to have something in his pocket and was going for it. She also hotly denied that she kicked him as he walked away. "If anybody says that I was booting him it is untrue," she blurted.

Thomas Hubble had the same treatment. When accused of violence by Mr Leigh he adamantly denied it. "I and my companions did not harass the prisoner and I did not hit him with a buckle!" Despite further questioning, Hubble maintained that he "saw a knife shining in his hand as he (the prisoner) went towards the lamp".

To further blacken the characters of the inhabitants of Fleet Street, Mr Leigh questioned Constable Pittaway about their conduct on the night. The officer had to admit that the crowd was very angry and that "the prisoner was struck twice by the crowd on the way to the station".

"What sort of people are they in Fleet Street?" asked Mr Leigh.
"They are not a very bright lot," said Constable Pittaway, at which the courtroom broke into laughter, much to the annoyance of the judge who warned everybody to keep quiet. "It is a low street," continued the officer. "I don't think we have a lower in Birmingham."

Mr Leigh knew that by questioning the morality of those living in Fleet Street he might win over the jury, so he continued by questioning Mr Jenkins, the borough surveyor. He also admitted that the area was bad and Fleet Street "a rather low place where after the closing of the public houses on a Saturday evening there would be a great deal of noise to the street".

A bad place where drunkenness and violence were rife? The very place where the poor unfortunate Thomas Russell found himself on the fatal evening? But did that prove that the occupants of Fleet Street were liars? Mr Leigh then set about calling witnesses which might prove just that.

Henry Weston was a clothier whose shop was in Great Western Street. He told the court that he had known Thomas Russell for 20 years through their business relationship and had always found him to be a "peaceable, thoroughly honest and upright man".

Russell would buy goods from Weston and sell them on. On 28th June the prisoner was in his shop at about 20 minutes to 11 and asked to borrow a pair of scissors to cut string from a parcel. As Weston did not have any scissors to hand he told the prisoner to use a knife to which Russell had replied, "You know I never carry a knife when I go out collecting on a Saturday."

"Why mention just a Saturday?" asked defence counsel.

"Well, sir, the prisoner said that he had a number of awkward customers that he collected money from on a Saturday immediately they had drawn their wages, just in case they spent them."

"And why did he say that you knew that he never carried a knife?" asked the judge.

"About two months ago the prisoner received some money and it got stuck between the knife blades. When he pulled the knife from his pocket the coins fell to the ground and he lost them. I had forgotten that he had said that he would never carry a knife again in case the same thing happened."

Weston added that Russell had left his shop just before 11 o'clock saying that he was off to collect money from a Mr Jefferson in Fleet Street.

William Jefferson had not been at home when the incident occurred, but his wife Selina had. She and her husband lived at 12 Fleet Street, next door to Mrs Cawley. On the evening of 28th June she saw Thomas Russell walk up the street and look at her front door and then at Mrs Cawley's. She knew him because her husband bought goods from his warehouse and paid for them weekly. She was about to go out and call to him when Mrs Cawley appeared and asked him what he was doing. Before Russell had time to reply Mrs Cawley began "hooting and quarrelling with him".

Mrs Jefferson went on to say that some boys appeared from the canal walk and joined in with the shouting at Russell. He tried to get away but they followed him up the street, along with Mrs Cawley. After some time Mrs Cawley returned and said to Selina Jefferson, 'I would not have gone up the street for a thousand pounds if I had known.' Later the witness realised that Mrs Cawley must have been referring to the stabbing. "She also told me, sir, that Thomas Hubble had taken off his belt and had beaten the old man on the head with it."

Selina Jefferson's evidence was supported by another resident of Fleet Street, Mary Johnson of number 18. She saw Russell on the night and he was carrying a parcel. She heard Mrs Cawley shout after him, but he had taken no notice and so she had grabbed him by his coat collar. He still took no notice so she called out for someone to stop him. At that point that a lot of boys came from the canal walk and mobbed him. At no time did she see Russell use a knife.

She went on to say that on the following Sunday she had heard Mrs Cawley talking to two other women. She had said, 'I am very glad I did not see it (the stabbing). I did not go any further than the Green Man.', a Fleet Street pub.

But Ann Cawley had said both at the magistates' hearing and at the trial that she witnessed the actual stabbing? The next witness was to throw even more doubt on the stories of the people of Fleet Street.

Sarah Griffiths lived in Sussex Street. She told the court that she was in Fleet Street on the fatal night and saw a crowd of about a dozen people. In the middle was Thomas Russell who was trying to escape. A woman in a light dress [Catherine Brookes] came up behind him, took him by the collar and dragged him back into the crowd. Immediately she heard the same woman scream "I am stabbed!" She was reaching over a boy's back, apparently trying to hit Russell whose hands were down in front of him. The boy whom Brookes had leaned over had his hand up as if he were going to strike someone, but the witness had not seen a knife.

Asked by the prosecution why she had not come forward before with the information, Sarah Griffiths said that she had been too frightened, "knowing what a rough and dangerous lot lived in that neighbourhood".

Having ascertained that some residents of Fleet Street could not really be trusted and had poor reputations, Mr Leigh went on to elaborate Thomas Russell's exemplary character. A series of witnesses enthused over what a good man he was. They included Detective Seal, who had known Russell for 20 years, Charles Salt, George Muntz and Thomas Grove, all businessmen, who had known Russell since the 1830's, and Mr Lloyd, a local J.P. who had employed Russell. They all said that the prisoner was 'a quiet and inoffensive man', and with that clearly established Mr Leigh, closed his defence.

It was left to Mr Justice Thesiger to sum up. He pointed to anomalies in the evidence. No knife had been found on the prisoner and he could not have thrown it away or Bruton would have seen him. Bruton said that he was never more than 5 yards from the prisoner in all of the chase. Mrs Cawley testified that she saw the stabbing and then said that she was nowhere near it. Witnesses for the prosecution said that they never used any violence on the prisoner, yet the defence witnesses say that they did. With these inconsistencies the judge felt that the only course was to find the prisoner not guilty, and the jury agreed.

Yet Caroline Brookes was killed by someone. The most likely culprit was the boy who had tried to strike Russell, but he was not to be found. Fleet Street closed ranks and refused to talk to the police. The law, so far as they were concerned, had let them down and they were not giving any more help.

Kicked to Death
(Longton 1887 - Daily Sentinel)

Forty year old Ralph Cotton had fallen on hard times. His last job was as a "back keeper" at the Wheat Sheaf Inn, Normacot Road, Longton, meaning that he helped the landlord with cellar work and filled in when he was absent. But he was forced to leave that job and found it almost impossible to find another except for casual work at the Talbot Inn, Commercial Street, which helped to pay for his lodgings there.

Lack of regular work had forced a separation with his family, but in September 1887 he moved back with his wife and three children at 6 Railway Terrace, East Vale on the outskirts of Longton. Everything seemed fine. On the morning of Wednesday 5th October 1887 he left the house, telling his wife that he was going to look for work and might stop off for a drink before he returned.

During the day he must have bumped into an old enemy, possibly someone he had barred from a pub, and there was a fight on some wasteground. Afterwards he refused to believe that anything was wrong with him and went to the Unicorn Inn, Sutherland Street, where he stayed just a few minutes. From there he went to the Railway Inn, East Vale, but again only stayed a short time.

When he arrived home at about 10 o'clock he was bleeding from his bottom, but after telling his wife that he had been in a fight he went to bed. The following day he stayed in bed until noon, then said he felt better and went out. It was not long before he was back home and in bed. His very worried wife called the doctor, but despite treatment Ralph Cotton died shortly before 5 am on Friday 7th October.

Doctor Coghlan had heard about the fight and immediately told the local police who started investigations to find the assailant. From the start though, their search was hampered by Cotton's stubborn refusal to name the attacker to either his wife or the doctor.

When the inquest opened on Monday 10th October at the Terrace Hotel, Longton the police had got no further with their inquiries. Mr Flint, the coroner from Uttoxeter, decided to continue the hearing in the hope that it might produce a lead for the police to follow.

Martha Cotton gave evidence that her husband had left home in good spirits at 9 o'clock on the Wednesday morning and had returned at 9.30 in the evening. He was perfectly sober to the point that she could not tell if he had had a drink, but he did not seem his usual self. When she asked what was the matter he said, "Something very serious", but would say no more.

ALLEDGED FATAL ASSAULT AT LONGDON.

A MAN KICKED TO DEATH.

Not wishing to upset him further, Martha had watched as he undressed and noticed blood on his clothes. He had discharged blood some months earlier and she thought it was a recurrence of that illness. But he bled throughout the night, and early on the Thursday she got him some brandy which eased his pain.

Still not realising the seriousness of the situation, she let her husband stay in bed all that morning without calling for the doctor. When he said that he felt better and would go out she relaxed because he promised to visit Mr Litchfield's, the chemist, for his usual prescription. But the chemist was closed and when Ralph returned he was much worse. It was then that Martha called the doctor.

A member of the jury asked why she left it so late. Martha said that her husband had suffered bleeding episodes before but recovered quickly. Despite her pleading her husband had refused to tell her any details of his fight or let her examine him.

"If I had known where he had been kicked," she said, "I would have contacted the doctor earlier."

Dr Coghlan also reflected on Mr Cotton's stubbornness. He told the hearing that Martha Cotton first called him between 3 and 4 o'clock on the Thursday afternoon. He had found the man to be very ill and noticed a utensil at the bedside half full of blood. "I found Mr Cotton reluctant to say anything," admitted the doctor, "but when I persisted he did admit to being kicked. However, he would say nothing of his attacker or why the fight had happened. All that the deceased would say was that it happened in Sutherland Street. When I still persisted the patient became angry and said, " Never mind; he has kicked me and I will kick him when I get better."

The doctor's examination showed that there was blood coming from the anus, which was badly bruised. "I treated him and then left, but when I returned on Friday he was already dead." In the post mortem he found that the rectum was ruptured and the arteries around it torn. The testicles were unharmed, but the urethra was severely lacerated. The cause of death was loss of blood because Ralph Cotton had been bleeding both internally and externally.

In answer to the coroner, Dr Coghlan said that death was not caused by "natural causes". It might have been caused by a fall, but it only if it had been onto a sharp object. He was as certain as he could be that the kick caused the death and that was why he told the police.

John Harrison, landlord of the Unicorn Inn, told the hearing that Cotton had come into his pub around 8 o'clock on the Wednesday evening. He was sober and ordered a glass of beer, but had only stayed for about five minutes. Harrison had not talked with him and presumed that Cotton wanted to get home quickly; he lived only 200 hundred yards away.

Thomas Palmer was landlord of the Railway Inn. He said that Ralph Cotton had called into his bar at about 9 o'clock that evening. After ordering a brandy and port wine he sat down, but after only six to seven minutes had left without speaking to anyone. He never heard Cotton complain, but when he left Palmer's attention was drawn to blood on his chair.

"Anxious that something was wrong, sir," Palmer said, "I visited his house at 7 am. Unfortunately he was still asleep and so I returned at 1.30 pm At that time he was awake but appeared very weak and so I gave him a glass of brandy."

Palmer told the court that he asked Cotton why he was so ill, and Cotton had told him about the fight and had then signalled to the sheets. The landlord noticed all the blood and saw where it was coming from. However, Cotton refused to talk about his attacker.

"When I persisted he said that he was feeling better and would like more brandy and water. I gave him some and then left, thinking he would be better with some rest. I was surprised to see him come into my public house shortly before 2 o'clock, but before long he complained that he was feeling worse and left. That was the last I saw of him alive, sir."

With no more witnesses the coroner asked Superintendent Evans if the police might be able to trace more of Ralph Cotton's movements on the fatal day, to which the officer said that given time they hoped to bring the killer to justice. So the inquest was adjourned, but by the time of the next hearing on Monday 17th October the police had simply drawn a blank.

Mr Flint spoke to the jury saying as there was no further evidence they would have to arrive at the best verdict possible based on evidence already produced. When questioned by a juror about the "fall" mentioned by the doctor, the coroner replied that "possibly it might have been a fall, but it was most probably a kick" that caused the fatal injury. That explained, the jury returned an "Open Verdict" in the hope that the police would eventually find the killer. They never did.

Muffled by Law
(Wednesbury 1869 - The Chronicle)

Fifty year old Eliza Bowen of The Green, Darlaston lived a hard and sad life made worse by drink. Husband William was serving nine month in goal for stealing chickens (not his first offence), while the previous September her eldest son had been sent to a reformatory. Another son, also William, had left home because he could not stand life there. Neighbours would have nothing to do with Eliza because of her wild behaviour, and so she became more lonely and isolated.

Eliza ranged far afield to drink and on the evening of Saturday, February 27th, 1869 she did so with one William Hall who was also known for unsavoury behaviour and bad temper. His first wife had left him due to his brutality. He had then taken up with a woman of "disreputable charm" but had finally remarried another, to whom he was equally brutal.

The two had obviously met at some stage during the evening and begun to drink heavily. Their behaviour caused a stir wherever they went making it easy for the police to track their movements.

The following morning John Turner, a waggoner, was on his way to clean out his horses stabled nearby when he came upon Eliza's corpse in Mud Lane, Wednesbury. She had been sexually attacked and horribly murdered. The police arrived and after several investigations of the area her body was taken to the Blue Ball Inn.

[Mud Lane does not appear in the 1881 census or on the Ordnance Survey map, so it was probably just a name used locally.]

The inquest was held at the Blue Ball on Monday, 1st March before Mr Hooper, the district coroner. Only two witnesses appeared at that time.

There are several pubs with the name Blue Ball in the Black Country. No doubt someone could explain its origin.

William Bowen identified his mother's corpse and outlined his family's poor history, adding that he had not seen his mother for many months.

The second witness was Henry Clay, a lamplighter. He had been on his way home down Mud Lane when he met John Turner who told him of a body in a nearby field and asked him to fetch the police. Clay thought they should check whether the person was dead and so they returned to the field. Eliza was certainly dead and covered with dirt, and the few ragged clothes which covered her limbs were disordered and torn.

A crowd had gathered and someone sent for Mr Kerr, the surgeon. Before he came Clay looked again at the body and saw that pieces of furnace cinder had been forced into the woman. He also found drag marks in the clay bank 26 yards away, as if she had been dragged across the road and then dumped in the field. It was there that he found her skirt.

At that point the coroner adjourned the inquest until 22nd March to await police enquiries.

A piece of torn muffler picked up at the murder scene and other investigations produced the name of William Hall. On Thursday 4th March Constables Walters and Evans visited Slater & Rubery, iron bridge and girder manufacturers at Darlaston where the 42 year old Hall worked as a striker. He travelled around Darlaston with the officers and was shown to several people who had seen Eliza on 27th February. Each of them recognised him as her companion on that evening.

After this he was taken to the local police station while Superintendent Holland and Sergeant Steele went to Hall's home, "a miserable cottage" at the Bull Piece, Darlaston. There they found the other part of the muffler which corresponded exactly with the one found at Mud Lane. As they took it from a drawer one of Hall's sons called out, "That's my father's muffler!" thinking they were trying to steal it.

Superintendent Holland charged Hall with the murder of Eliza Bowen and he was picked out in an identity parade by a Mrs Reader as the man she had seen with Eliza on Saturday 27th February. Closer examination of Hall's clothes revealed slight patches of clayey mud, similar to that found on the road where the struggle happened.

On Friday 5th March Hall was taken before the magistrates. Although it was well known that the court would not sit until 2.00 pm the police station was surrounded long before 9.00 am. Such was local disgust at the crime that many people wanted to catch a glimpse of the (alleged) despicable villain, and the police had trouble in preventing the court from being overcrowded. Hall made matters worse for himself by smiling as he entered.

Before Magistrates Marshall, Davis and Williams he was formally charged and pleaded not guilty. After hearing the evidence from Holland the magistrates had no difficulty in remanding Hall to Stafford Goal until further investigations had taken place. As he was taken down Mrs Hall cried out, "Oh lad, if you know aught about it, do tell me!" to which Hall replied that he knew nothing.

> **THE SHOCKING MURDER OF A WOMAN AT WEDNESBURY.**
> **THE SUPPOSED MURDERER IN CUSTODY.**

On Wednesday 10th March and Wednesday 17th March the same magistrates sat for the committal hearing.

Henry Clay and William Bowen repeated their evidence to the inquest and John Turner, who found the body, gave his account of the Sunday morning.

Next came Constable Walters. He had reached the scene at 7.55 am and found Eliza Bowen's skirt lying on the right side of the lane. With it were three penny pieces. Constable Evans found the piece of muffler close by, then both officers examined the corpse before taking it to the Blue Ball Inn.

Daniel Kerr, the surgeon, had arrived in Mud Lane just before the policemen and had made an initial examination of the body. It was lying parallel to the fence and about a yard away from it. Eliza Bowen was lying on her back with her arms drawn upwards and slightly crossed. The knees were fixed upon the thigh and drawn upwards and to the left. Her bonnet was tied behind and resting on the front of the neck.

After the corpse was taken to the pub Kerr looked at it with his assistant, Mr Rix. There was an abrasion over the right eye and on the cheek bone from which blood had flowed. A shawl was fastened tightly around the woman's neck by a brooch, which was behind the neck. Unfastening the brooch Mr Kerr found a piece of string to which was attached a small bag containing three penny pieces. There were no injuries to the arms or chest.

The surgeon went on to describe the horrific injuries to the lower part of the corpse. They were so terrible that *The Chronicle* refused to print them. All they reported was that "certain parts of her body were frightfully lacerated and swollen and the surgeon extracted seventeen pieces of cinder and one piece of brick from the body. One of those, which was deeply imbedded, was a conical piece about 3½ inches long and about 3 to 4 inches in circumference, while another was 2 inches long and 1½ inches wide."

Mr Kerr told the court that the cause of death must have been the forcible insertion of the stones and the shock it caused. Death was probably accelerated by exposure. In his opinion the stones must have been inserted before death and "were sufficient alone to have ultimately caused death."

With the crowd in the court room reeling from the description of the corpse Superintendent Holland took the witness box. He described his preliminary investigations then described Hall's arrest. "Having had the prisoner brought to the station I laid the two pieces of scarf on the desk before him and read out the charge. He turned very pale and replied, "I know nothing about it." They had arrested Hall because in all his statements to the police he had lied.

It was left to Sergeant Steele to give evidence about those interviews and he told the court how he and other police officers had examined the body and then traced Hall's movements on the fatal evening.

He asked Hall if he had been in the Victoria, Butcroft, owned by William Griffiths, and Hall said that he had not. When he asked him if he had been in the Manchester or "Fourpenny House" that evening Hall had replied that he had, but had been alone.

Next Hall was asked if he had been in the Green Dragon, Market Place, Wednesbury and remembered a glass being broken for which he paid 3 pence [1.25p]. Again Hall denied being there but added that he had been in Mr Laxton's at the bottom of Market Place and drunk two pints of ale.

When asked who he was with Hall insisted that he had been alone and that he got home between 11 and 12 o'clock. Asked if he accompanied anyone home that night, Hall first said that his wife had been with him, but then changed his mind and said that she was at home all evening.

Sergeant Steele said that he had taken Hall to the Victoria at Butcroft where two witness (Joseph Burford and Charles Orton) identified him as the man in the pub with a woman.

Steele then told the court that he had taken the prisoner to Wednesbury Police Station where his clothes were examined. When mud was found on the waistcoat which corresponded with that found in Mud Lane Hall was charged with the murder of Eliza Bowen.

Because of all of his lies the police were convinced that Hall had murdered the poor woman, so they went on to show the court what a terrible liar he was by producing a succession of witnesses who would swear to Hall's movements and companions on the evening of Saturday 27th February.

Joseph Burford and Charles Orton said that Hall and Eliza had been in the Victoria pub just after 9.30 on the Saturday. The woman paid for her own half pint and the prisoner paid for his, handing over a half crown [2s-6d], receiving 2s-3d change [11.25p]. The prisoner said to the deceased, "Drink, my wench." which she did and they both left together.

John Pynn and William Conncok were waiters at the Green Dragon, Wednesbury. They said that Hall came in at about 11.05 with Eliza and another little man. The prisoner had a pint then called for a jug of ale which the three drank from until 11.35. The woman broke a cup [mug] but said she had no money to pay for it and was asked to leave. Hall had then finished his ale and deliberately broken his mug, for which he paid 3 pence.

"What of the little man?" asked the magistrate.
"I did not know him, sir," replied Pynn, "but I would recognise him if I saw him. I did not see him leave with the prisoner and the woman, but he had gone after the disturbance."

Joseph Cotton was in the Green Dragon when the woman was turned out and he had left minutes later. As he walked up the High Bullen (a street in Wednesbury) he noticed the woman and Hall going up the steps of the Horse & Jockey which is on the road from the Green Dragon to Darlaston. Cotton was sure that the two were alone.

Having placed Hall with Eliza in the various pubs in the area, the prosecution called witnesses who saw the couple later that evening, especially in Mud Lane.

Eliza Reader, wife of Charles Reader, a bolt forger from Darlaston Green, described how she and her husband, her brother Joseph Rogers and his wife had left her mother's house in Earp's Lane, Wednesbury at 10 minutes past 12 to walk to Hall End where her brother lived.

As they went along Mud Lane they saw a man and a woman. The woman was crouching down and the man was standing and appeared to be looking for something. As they neared the pair her husband said to the man, "Old fellow, you have a tidy nerve to have a woman here at this time of night." The man did not reply.

When questioned Mrs Reader confessed that she had not seen the man's face as he had turned away when they approached, but she was sure it was William Hall. She had not seen the woman's face either but knew that she was small and dirty, and when the murder was reported she knew that it must be the same woman.

Charles Reader and Martha Rogers appeared to corroborate Mrs Reader's evidence and when Joseph appeared he told much the same story. However, he added that after he had walked to the end of Mud Lane with his sister and brother in law he returned home and then he and his wife went back into Mud Lane to check on the couple. At that time the woman was on the ground and the man had hold of her hands and appeared to be trying to get her up. Like the other three witnesses he did not see the man's face.

Eleven year old Jonah Dutton from Hall End had gone to fetch beer for his father. In Trouse Lane he saw a man and a woman in the middle of the road between Old Park Terrace and Mr Sansome's public house. He clearly saw the face of Eliza Bowen but did not see the man's face. Young Dutton heard the woman say, "Let me go this road, it is the best for me." The man replied, "No, you come this road, it is the best for you." They then went up towards Hall End.

Samuel Kendrick was coming from Falling's Heath and into Wednesbury by way of the Black Horse when he saw a man and woman coming out of an opening in Mud Lane. They came down the field by the Tommy Shop to the lane. He could not see their faces but the man wore a low billycock [hat], a dark jacket and a lightish pair of trousers. The woman was small and wore light clothes and a bonnet. Both seemed drunk as they walked away up Mud Lane. The time was about 8 minutes past 12.

Then the evidence turned to the muffler, a piece of which was found at the murder scene. John Critch said that he knew Hall well and had seen him wearing a muffler or scarf like the one produced in court as recently as a month ago.

Joseph Taylor said that he had known William Hall for about four months and had been out with him twice. He had seen him wearing a muffler like the one in court since the Christmas period.

Elizabeth Wilkes said that Hall had lived next door to her and her husband, Joseph, for two weeks before the murder. On the Wednesday after the murder she noticed Mrs Hall washing. When she pegged out the clothes the witness saw two scarfs on the line; a red and black one was torn at the end and was like the scarf produced in court.

Asked why she was so certain about the muffler, Mrs Wilkes replied, "It was in my road when I went to the water tub and on that account I noticed it. One end was hanging in shreds."

With the evidence against Hall completed the magistrates asked him if he would like to call witnesses on his behalf when the hearing resumed on Friday 19th. His barrister, Mr Sheldon, said that he would, but strangely, on the Friday he declined to question them. Given the weight of evidence the magistrates had no option but to remand Hall for trial at the Stafford Assizes.

During all this time the coroner, Mr Hooper, had been waiting to resume his inquest, but because of the magistrates' court proceedings he had not found a suitable time. When he did finally secured a date Hall was already in Stafford Goal awaiting trial and was not allowed to attend the inquest.

Despite Hooper's many protests, including writing to and visiting the Home Office, Hall was still not allowed to leave the goal. The coroner was concerned by the point of law that everyone has the right to attend a hearing at which they are accused of something. More importantly, they have the right to question any prosecution witnesses. As far as Mr Hooper was concerned Hall was being denied those rights which made the whole legality of the inquest doubtful.

Eventually the coroner was forced to hold his inquest on 27th May, but as at the other postponed hearings, he made his feelings about the absence of Hall very clear to the jury.

All the witnesses seen at the magistrates' court were brought again to give evidence before the coroner and his jury. Each one repeated their evidence without adding anything new then the coroner addressed the jury.

Whether or nor Mr Hooper might be accused of prejudice because of his dealings with the magistrates' and Home Office we can't tell from the newspaper reports, but in summing up the case he did labour certain points which just might have prejudiced the jury. At all events, Mr Hooper wanted to put some sort of case for Hall.

First he stressed that the various witnesses in the Green Dragon gave differing accounts of whether Hall was with the woman or not and whether she had left with him or not. Secondly, despite witnesses saying that they saw the two together outside the various public houses and heading towards Mud Lane or in the lane, no one could say that they had actually seen Hall's face. Most did not even see Eliza Bowen's face either, but had speculated that it must be her after they had heard of the crime. Finally, there had been little evidence to show that the muffler belonged to the prisoner, but more importantly, no one had seen him wearing it on the fatal night.

With those points stressed the jury retired. After an hour the coroner ordered that the jury be "locked up" until a verdict had been reached. However, after another hour and a half they asked to see him and at 8.30 pm the coroner asked the foreman if they had reached a decision.

"We have not," came his reply.
"May I ask if there is any probability of your doing so?" enquired Mr Hooper.
"Not in the least," replied the Foreman.

The coroner had no option but to bind over the jury and the witnesses to appear at the Assizes.

The main function of an inquest was (and still is) to decide the time, place and cause of death. However, under long since abandoned law, if the inquest jury decided that a particular person was responsible for the death they could name them and commit them for full trial at the Assize Court by issuing a Bill of Indictment. This had the same effect as a committal for trial by magistrates. In this case the magistrates' had decided to commit but the inquest jury had not.

On Wednesday 21st July Mr Hooper and the jury appeared before Mr Justice Smith who was to preside over the trial. The coroner discussed the inquest jury's failure to reach a verdict and sought the judge's advice. He ruled that the jury must only present a Bill if they were all of a mind that the prisoner was guilty.

On 28th July the trial opened. Although the inquest jury had issued no Bill, Hall had been committed by the magistrates and the trial could go ahead. Much to the horror of all those present at the Assizes, the judge discharged Hall and he walked free from custody on the Thursday.

Infuriatingly, neither *The Chronicle* nor the other newspapers reported anything which might explain this decision. Was the judge convinced that the case was so prejudiced by the conflicting results from the lower courts that Hall could not be given a fair trail? There have been many cases in which a full trial has gone ahead without an inquest Bill so its mere absence could not have been the reason.

The public were horrified at this outcome to the case and the police were dumbfounded. They were positive that they had their murderer. However, according to law Eliza Bowen's killer was still at large and the crime remains unsolved to this day.

A Life for Two Farthings
(Wolverhampton 1902 - Express & Star)

At 5.55 am on Monday 22nd December 1902, a wintery morning when the sooty darkness was total, inky and absorbing, John Jones, blacksmith of 31 South Street, Bushbury, felt his way down unlighted streets to work.

Finding it difficult even to keep his footing, he finally reached the secluded road which ran beside the factory of Danks & Walkers near the Victoria Basin of the Great Western Railway in Wolverhampton. Almost there, he quickened his pace only to stumble and fall over what he thought was "a heap of rags". Lighting a match he found himself lying near a woman who was face down and looked quite dead.

Terrified, he raced off to fetch the police and returned shortly afterwards with Constable Moran. Having told the officer how he came by the corpse he went on to work while Moran waited near the body for Inspector Purchase to arrive.

What they discovered was gruesome. The victim's clothes had been torn open leaving the chest completely bare. Her dress and petticoat had been torn right down to the waistband, suggesting rape. The body was badly marked. There was a very black eye in a seriously bruised face with the nose and mouth badly swollen. The right wrist was badly bruised and there were bruise marks on the left knee. The woman was covered in dried blood, showing that the attack had taken place some hours before.

The area around the body was splashed with blood, including one large patch some 12 by 18 inches wide on the corrugated iron wall of a nearby building. Close to that bloodstain lay the woman's hat. As if the injuries had not been enough to kill her, the woman's face had been pressed into the soil in an attempt to suffocate her.

After examining the area thoroughly the policemen took the body to the mortuary where it was examined more fully by Sergeant Johnson, the officer attached to the coroner's office.

He recognised the woman immediately though he could not remember her name. She was well known to the local police as a prostitute who lodged at 23 Stafford Street, Wolverhampton. To help in his identification he found a pocket stitched into the skirt which held a purse containing two pawn tickets. They were dated October 6th and 7th and bore the name of Jane Doley.

To make indentification absolutely certain the landlady of the Stafford Street lodgings was summoned to the mortuary and she confirmed that the corpse was indeed Jane.

The inquest opened on Tuesday 22nd December 1902 at the Town Hall, Wolverhampton and at this stage the coroner wanted only to confirm the victim's identity and the cause of death. The only witness was Richard Doley, Jane's estranged husband. Hearing rumours that his ex-wife had been murdered he had gone to the police and helped identify the corpse.

Trying to spare the poor man's feelings, the coroner, Mr Willcock, asked him to give just brief details of his relationship with Jane. Richard Doley told the hearing that he lived at 24 Wood Street, Cannock Road, Wolverhampton with his daughter. His other child, a son, was away in the army. Although a fitter by trade, shortage of work had lead him to take a job as a pump operator in a local mine.

Clearly distressed, he said that his marriage had broken down completely some eighteen months before when his wife had left him and the children. Since then he had rarely seen her, the last time was Easter, but he knew that she lived in Stafford Street. He had been told by neighbours that she was "living a life of shame" and so he determined never to see her again.

Asked by the coroner whether he had proof of her behaviour he admitted that he had nothing definite, but so many people had reported on it that he found it difficult to disbelieve them all. The coroner was moved by Richard's distress and adjourned for two weeks so that the police might make every effort. "to see that the miscreant, whoever he or she was, could be brought to justice".

By the time of the next hearing on 6th January 1903 the police had arrested a man named Martin Brown who was a strong suspect on four counts. Firstly, he had known the victim; secondly, he was in the habit of wearing neckerchiefs similar to one found at the murder scene; thirdly, he was vague about his movements on the night of the crime; and lastly, he had been overheard admitting that he had killed a woman, though he had not mentioned her name.

Unfortunately for both police and coroner, the inquest hearings were to be plagued by problems, not the least of which were the witneses, which at times made them seem more like a pantomime than a court.

At the start one of the jurymen was missing, a Mr Earp, who appeared seventeen minutes late. When asked why he simply replied, "I did not know it was that late". Annoyed, the coroner fined Earp 10 shillings [50p] and angrily told him to sit down.

Martin Brown did not help matters when he stoutly refused to enter the witness box, as was his right, but insisted on questioning a witnesses from his seat. Mr Willcock fought hard to keep discipline while trying to conduct an impartial hearing.

That dealt with, the first witness was Ellen Ireson, manageress and book keeper of the lodging house at 23 Stafford Street. She had known Jane Doley for the last twelve months as a lodger. She also knew Brown who had lodged at her house, but not within the last four months. She said that Brown had known the dead woman and on Saturday afternoons they had often gone out together for a drink to the Four Ashes Inn, especially when Brown had his wages.

Brown often visited her lodgings to see various occupants, the last time being a fortnight before Christmas Day when he had visited a lodger named Thornton.

Asked by the coroner how Martin Brown usually dressed, particularly "about the neck", she had no hesitation in saying, "He usually wore a dark muffler, sometimes dark blue. The neckerchief was not silk, but a cheap cotton one. He did not wear a showy one, but sometimes wore one with stripes."

Interested to know why Ireson should be so adamant that they were not "showy" the coroner said, "Why did you use that expression showy? Slightly confused she replied, "I used to wash his neckerchiefs and shirts."

Still puzzled the coroner continued, "Were you told that the neckerchief found at the crime was a showy one?" To which she replied, "A policeman, Sergeant Nixon, showed me the neckerchief and asked me if I recognised it."

Mr Willcock was unhappy that Ellen Ireson might have been fed information but allowed her to continue. She said that Jane Doley was in the lodgings talking to her at 9.40 on the fatal night and said that she was going to meet a friend. She left the house and headed down Little Lane. Jane had not named the friend but said that she would be no more than half an hour.

The dead woman had shown her a 2 shilling piece and two farthings and at first asked Ellen to keep them for her but had then changed her mind. [2 shillings = 10p, a farthing was a quarter of an old penny worth in modern terms about 1 tenth of 1p, if you can imagine that.] Jane Doley had also told Ellen that the previous night a man had given her the two farthings saying that they were sixpences [2½p]. It had been dark and she had not realised at the time, but she was going to find that man and tell him.

Before Ireson left the witness box Martin Brown exercised his right to ask her questions, and once again she insisted that Brown had taken Jane out for drinks.

"You tell an untruth!" Brown shouted. "I have never taken her out." Startled, Ellen Ireson replied, "Mrs Doley was sewing buttons on your shirt and you said you would take her out for a drink as a reward."
Heatedly Brown retorted, "Can you tell me when the day was you say I asked her?"

Then Ireson, confused and feeling threatened, admitted, "No, I cannot tell or mention any particular Saturday, but Mrs Doley had never sewn buttons on for other lodgers."

Fearing that his hearing might get out of hand, the coroner stopped the cross examination.

The next witness was Annie Duffy, an intelligent girl who lived at 26 Herbert Street, Wolverhampton. She told the court that she left home on Sunday 21st

December making for Victoria Basin to mind her sister's children. The family lived on a boat in the basin called the *Blythe*.

At about 9.15 that night after her sister and husband had gone out she heard screams and cries of "murder" which seemed to come from near the office of Danks & Walker. After the screams she heard a woman moaning and footsteps leaving the area. Too frightened to go outside, Annie waited until her sister came home and told her about it. It was the following day that she heard of the murder.

Questioned by the coroner about the exact time, Annie was insistent that it could have been no later than 9.15, yet according to Ellen Ireson Jane Doley had not left the lodging until nearly 10.00 pm.

If Annie Duffy set the courtroom buzzing the next witness caused a sensation. Thomas Nash, a shoemaker, was living at Hinde's Lodging House in Piper's Row on 27th December, one week after the murder. At 10.30 that evening he was in the closet [toilet] at the rear of the house when he overheard a man say, "I've killed a woman." Startled, he listened closely and heard the man repeat it, then add, "I don't know what to do."

Curiosity forced him to enter the room from where the voice had come and he found Martin Brown. His hands were at the back of his head and he was swaying to and fro and crying.

"Are you sure?" asked the coroner.
"Yes, sir," replied Nash. "He repeated it to me."
"What did you do next?"
"I said, "Are you going mad, man? What is the matter with you?" Brown then said, "A ------ like you could not have put her in like I have done."
"Did you believe him?" the coroner asked.
"He was drunk at the time, sir, but I went and told the police exactly what he had told me."

[Do you believe Nash? Brown's behaviour as he describes it a week after the murder seems very theatrical, talking to himself with his hands to his head. It seems more the way an actor of the day would play a murderer than the way people really behaved.]

Turning to the prisoner the coroner asked if he would like to question the witness. Brown declined and refused to give evidence himself but shouted, "I know I was drunk that night, but I don't acknowledge saying that!"

The next witness seemed to support Brown's claim. George York was a labourer and another lodger at Hinde's. He had been staying there for some time and had become a friend of Martin Brown. On the evening of 21st December he was at the lodgings all night. Brown had left with another man whose name he could not remember, but the two had returned at about 9.45. Brown had asked York to fetch some beer, which he did, and Brown and his companion sat and drank it before going to bed.

Asked by the coroner asked what Brown was wearing that night, York said he wore a white neckerchief all day, but he was not sure about the colour of his shirt.

"Did he change his shirt when he came in?" asked the coroner.
"No, sir, not to my knowledge," replied York.
"What did he sleep in?" asked Mr Willcock.
"I should think he took his shirt off," replied York. "It is the custom in lodging houses to sleep with nothing on."

The coroner then asked York for the names of other people in the lodging on 21st December who might corroborate his evidence. Hesitantly, York said that he thought the men who slept in the room with Brown were Nibbs and Fellows, but he could not be certain.

Turning to the events of 27th December as described by Nash, the coroner asked York what he knew. York was adamant that he had seen Brown in the kitchen and he seemed quite drunk, but at no time had he heard Brown admit to killing a woman. However, he did have a cut over his right eye.

York's hesitation in naming the other lodgers might seem strange, but Victorian lodging houses harboured many unsavoury characters who might only stay for short periods. Book keeping and visitors lists were often misleading as the owners were more interested in payment than the characters of their customers. With the constant flow of changing lodgers it was almost impossible to be certain of times and dates, yet the next witness was adamant about her evidence.

Louisa Silvester acted as deputy at Hinde's Lodging House and was there on the weekend of 21st December. Her main duty had been to collect rent for the rooms and she told the court that Brown had paid for both Saturday and Sunday and paid for York as well.

She added that Brown had not been in the lodging all night on 21st December and had returned only on the morning of the 22nd. She said that she remembered it clearly because she had asked him where he had stayed and he said that he had spent the night at his sister's. But she added that she had washed Martin Brown's shirts and was certain there was no blood on them.

Who was telling the truth, Nash, York, Silvester? York was recalled, but insisted that Brown had been at the lodging that evening. As to Brown paying his rent (and giving him a motive to lie), he said that Miss Silvester was mistaken because York had given Brown the money to pay for the room. She must have thought that Brown paid out of his own money.

So far the case had become bogged down with Brown's movements on 21st December but no one had seen blood on him. At this stage the coroner called Dr Wolverton, the police surgeon.

He gave a graphic account of Jane Doley's injuries and the blood which had spread all over her and the surrounding area. He suggested that the victim had probably lain down herself to prepare for "the immoral act", suggested by her clothing having been pulled up to the upper legs and the neckerchief placed around her thighs, but instead had been savagely attacked and kicked as she lay there.

Dr Cholmesley who assisted with the examination agreed that the victim received her bruises through being severely kicked. Both doctors agreed that she had not been raped and that death was caused by the sudden shock of her terrible injuries. Asked about the state of the killer, they agreed that the attack was so frenzied that he or she could hardly have escaped being covered in blood.

No one had detected the slightest trace of blood on the accused, so had the police arrested the wrong man? By law Martin Brown could not be compelled to give evidence, but the coroner asked him if he would like to and Brown insisted that he did.

He was a labourer, he said, his main work being to empty coal boats. On 18th December he had been paid and returned to his lodgings at Hinde's where he had been for four weeks. Despite having his own wages, his friend York paid for the weekend's rent because it was his turn. Louisa Silvester must have thought that he, Brown, had paid himself because it was he who handed over the money.

On Sunday 21st December he got up at 8 o'clock and had breakfast with York. He did not leave the lodgings until 1 o'clock when he went over to the Barley Mow to see a man who had sent for him. They shared three pints of beer and then returned to the lodgings at 2 o'clock, where he had something to eat and stayed in all afternoon. At 8 o'clock in the evening he went back to the Barley Mow and met the same friend. They drank four pints each and then both returned to the lodgings at about 9.30. He went to bed just before 10.00 after sharing another pint with the friend.

The following morning York rose at 5 o'clock to go to work and he, Brown, was up at 7. He had breakfast and left for work, arriving at Cane Wharf just before 8.00 am. Then, as if completely satisfied with his account, Brown breathed in deeply, stared at the jury and said, "That's the end of that", assuming there would be no questions and he would be instantly dismissed.

The coroner had other thoughts.
"Why would Louisa Silvester say that you were out all night on 21st December?" asked Mr Willcock.
All that Brown would say was that she was lying or at best confused.

"And what of the night of 27th December?" continued the coroner. "Is it true what the man said about you in the house?" Brown admitted to being drunk that evening but denied saying anything about killing a woman.
"Then why should he say such a thing?" pressed Mr Willcock.
"Because he was the sort of man capable of doing anything!" Brown shouted.
"Why do you say that?" inquired the coroner.
"Because he's rough and ready like most of us!" Brown retorted.

It was late and the coroner felt he was getting nowhere, so he adjourned the hearing until Thursday 8th January. By the time that hearing opened the police had found further witnesses whom they hoped might throw more light on the case and even prove Brown's guilt.

William Gallear, another lodger at Hinde's Lodging House, had been there for three months and knew Martin Brown well. He said that on Sunday 21st December Brown was at the house all morning until 1 o'clock when he was called out. He came back at about 2.30 and stayed in until 8 o'clock. Gallear was certain that Brown was back before 10.00. Gallear had gone to bed at 10.00 and distinctly remembered seeing Brown in the kitchen at that time.

Asked about about Brown's clothes and in particular neckerchiefs, Gallear said that he always wore them but he was not sure of their colour. He said that Brown knew Jane Doley but he had never seen them together.

Gallear said that on 27th December he saw Brown enter the house between 10.00 and 11.00 pm and he looked as though he had drunk "a drop of beer". He also had a cut over one eye which was bleeding.

The next witness was Thomas Newell, another lodger, who cast more doubt on Louisa Silvester's evidence. He was certain that Brown was in the house on the night of 21st December because he remembered seeing him as he, Newell, went to bed.

The case against Brown seemed to be collapsing, but the police thought they had two key witnesses.

Ellen Murphy of 6 Southampton Street, which was opposite to where Jane Doley was found, had told them that Brown visited her and her husband at 4.00 pm on Saturday 26th December. He was drunk and said he had no money to pay for his lodgings. She had fed him and allowed him to stay the night, but reprimanded him for his way of living. She had accused him of murdering "that woman" and Brown had not denied it. She also told the police that her husband had told her to be quiet in case they got into trouble.

Much to police dismay, when Ellen Murphy gave evidence she denied ever saying anything of the sort to Brown.

"But why tell the police anything?" queried the coroner. After an awkward silence she said, "I must have been confused at the time, sir."

Likewise her husband, John, also denied ever hearing his wife say anything to Brown.
"Why then would the police invent such a story?" demanded an exasperated coroner.
"They've got it on the brain down there (meaning the police) and they don't know what they're talking about!" retorted Murphy.

Despite several attempts to get John Murphy to alter his testimony, he would not. Thoroughly disgusted, the coroner shouted at Murphy to "Stand down" and once more closed the hearing until 15th January.

That third hearing was to prove just as frustrating for Mr Willcock. Giving evidence was one William Cook, a commercial traveller of Randolph Place, Hordern Road. He had been at the Talbot Hotel on 10th January shortly before one 1 o'clock and had bragged that he "could put his hands on three men, each of whom had kicked at the murdered woman". Unfortunately he had bragged in front of a Mr Edwards, a member of the jury, who immediately told the police who questioned Cook and forced him to attend the hearing.

A rather sorry looking Cook then had to admit that he was merely repeating gossip.

"Do you have any knowledge at all in connection with this case?" demanded the coroner. To which a red faced Cook admitted. "I have not the slightest knowledge of anything. I know nothing about it."

Severely reprimanded by the coroner, Cook was told that he was lucky not to be brought before the court himself for his behaviour and was instantly dismissed.

Trying to make some sense of the conflicting evidence Mr Willock called Louisa Silvester again, and she maintained her story that Brown was absent from the lodgings over the night of 21st December.

William Fellows, then lodging at 13 Dale Street, said that he had shared a bedroom with Brown on 21st December. He was at the lodgings until 7 o'clock in the evening when he left and went to the New Inns at Horsley Fields. Brown was at the lodgings all of the time. When he returned Brown was there and still there when he went to bed. When George York awoke at 5 o'clock the next morning he disturbed Fellows who remembered seeing Brown in bed at the time.

The case was going nowhere and Mr Willcock had had enough. He told the jury that most witnesses had proved unreliable, as might be expected from such who frequented lodging houses. However, the police had failed to prove Brown's guilt, especially failing to produce any evidence of blood stained clothing. He must advise the jury to return a verdict of "Not Guilty". In they end they found "that the woman had died from shock, consequent upon her injuries, and that she was murdered by some person or persons unknown".

In his closing remark the coroner said, "Time may bring forth something which has not been brought to light and the person will perhaps have to answer when evidence is forthcoming". Neither time nor anything else ever did. The only twist in the sorry saga came in the Magistrates Court on 19th January when Louisa Silvester changed her story and said that Brown had been at the lodging on 21st December.

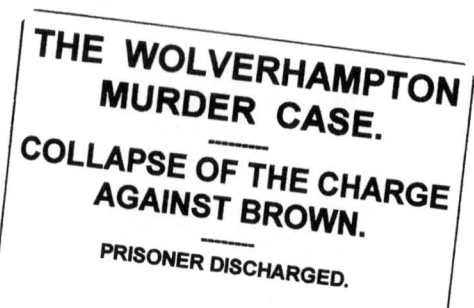

Who killed Jane Doley? Had she confronted the stranger who gave her two farthings instead of two sixpences? Had he persuaded her to have sex again after which he would pay her in full, but instead he had kicked her to death to save his reputation? If so, what a price Jane Doley paid.

Murders

by Barrie Roberts
Midland Murders & Mysteries (ISBN 1-898136-14-9)
Murder in the Midlands (ISBN 1-898136-19-X)

Barrie Roberts's two collections of murders draw on cases from 1760 to the 1960s committed in all corners of the Midlands. Meet the boy who stole bones from a graveyard, the detective who didn't see a murderer board the train, the housekeeper dead in a locked room, the lodger who fell for his landlady and the rich brewer who didn't kill his lover. Some murders were never solved but one killer was caught by chance after 25 years. Greed and jealousy, guns, knives and poison all appear in these absorbing stories.

by Anthony Hunt
Accident, Manslaughter or Murder? (ISBN 1 898136 20 3)

Tony Hunt's historical research into copies of Victorian newspapers lead him to retell these murder cases from their detailed reports of trials and inquests. Why was Thomas's Hollier's horse wandering loose in a lane, who threw the body down Shaft 7, how did the marble get into the empty pistol and what was the sinister influence of Lame Joe Marshall? Many coroner's inquests came to no clear conclusion about deaths and many trials ended in mystery in an age of poverty, cobbles and gas light.

£8.45 each, post free in UK

QuercuS
**The Garden House, 67 Cliffe Way, Warwick
CV34 5JG UK**

Tel/fax 01926 776363
john@walkwaysquercus.co.uk
www.walkwaysquercus.co.uk

..the Weird..

? *"I can only describe it as a glass pyramid about three inches high, and its one side was shimmering as if charged with electricity."*

? *One day he said, "There's a funny bloke in my bedroom. He walked up to me, took off his top hat and asked me where the hall stand was."*

? *"Suddenly the bed covers began ... going up and down. By the side of Stephanie's bed was a ... large toy snake ... made from fluffy fabric with a red felt tongue. Stephanie slowly raised her hands in the air and the snake was moving in and out of her fingers."*

? *"The train had a Midland side tank engine of the Johnson design, LMS 3F No. 47344, and three coaches ... As it went past it didn't make a sound."*

Anne Bradford and Barrie Roberts's three books tell mystifying stories from ordinary people describing their own experiences at home, at work and at leisure. Find out what Alan heard in a carriage on the Severn Valley Railway, what Keith saw in the Erdington phone box and the curious habit of the late William Elton of Stafford.

Midland Ghosts & Hauntings (ISBN 1 898136 05 X)
Midland Spirits & Spectres (ISBN 1 898136 16 5)
Strange Meetings (ISBN 1 898136 21 1)
£8.45 each, post free in UK

QuercuS

The Garden House, 67 Cliffe Way, Warwick
CV34 5JG UK

Tel/fax 01926 776363
john@walkwaysquercus.co.uk
www.walkwaysquercus.co.uk